NOT
GUILTY

NOT GUILTY

Twelve Black Men Speak Out

on Law, Justice, and Life

Edited by Jabari Asim

 Amistad

An Imprint of HarperCollinsPublishers

HarperCollins books may be purchased for educational, business, or sales promotional use. For information, please write: Special Markets Department, Harper-Collins Publishers Inc., 10 East 53rd Street, New York, NY 10022.

"Justice" reprinted from *The Collected Poems of Langston Hughes* by Langston Hughes, copyright @ 1994 by The Estate of Langston Hughes. Used by permission of Alfred A. Knopf, a division of Random House, Inc.

FIRST EDITION

Designed by Nicola Ferguson

Printed on acid-free paper

Library of Congress Cataloging-in-Publication Data
Not guilty : twelve Black men speak out on law, justice, and life /
edited by Jabari Asim.
p. cm.
ISBN 0-06-018538-4
1. Discrimination in criminal justice administration—
United States.   2. Discrimination in justice administration—United States.
3. Discrimination in law enforcement—
United States.   4. Racism—United States.   5. United States—Race relations.   I. Asim, Jabari.

HV9950 N67   2001
364'.089'96073—dc21   2001022779

01   02   03   04   WBC/RRD   10   9   8   7   6   5   4   3   2   1

For Liana, who has always believed

ACKNOWLEDGMENTS

Heartfelt gratitude to all of the following: My parents; my siblings; my wife and children; my colleagues at the *Washington Post,* especially Marie Arana, Jonathan Yardley, Michael Dirda, Kunio Francis Tanabe, Nina King, David Nicholson, Jennifer Howard, Dennis Drabelle, Brian Jacomb, Chris Lehmann, Mary Morris, Christopher Schoppa, Ednamae Sorti, Jay Fernandez, Carolyn Ruff Spellman, Lonnae O'Neal Parker, and Marcia Davis; Valerie Boyd; Ira B. Jones; Vaness Sgambati; Andrea M. Wren; Sylvester Brown Jr.; Victoria Anton; Samuel G. Freedman; the Black House Brothers: Mark Arnett, Mark Scott, Phil Neely, Leon Rallings, and Ayton Taylor; Jamel Richardson and Tracey Tisdale-Richardson; Carman Savage and family; James and Elsie Richardson; Kevin Powell; Fred McKissack Jr.; Afi Afuru; Eugene B. Redmond; Shirley LeFlore; my teachers, Betty Hayden, Harriette Hamilton, Gloria Griffero, Ernestine McKellar, the late Dorothy Greiwe, Njoki McElroy, Gayle Pemberton, the late Leon Forrest, the late Ulysses Duke Jenkins; my friends at Vertigo Books, especially Bridget Warren and Todd Stewart; my agent, Joy Harris; my editor, Charles F. Harris; and not least, the contributors to this volume, for all their discipline, dedication, critical intelligence, and heartfelt eloquence: you humble and inspire me.

That Justice is a blind goddess
Is a thing to which we black are wise.
Her bandage hides two festering sores
That once perhaps were eyes.

—"Justice" by Langston Hughes

CONTENTS

Introduction: Twelve Moods for Justice   *xiii*
JABARI ASIM

Just Another "Nigga": Reflections on Black
Masculinity and Middle-Class Identity   *1*
MARK ANTHONY NEAL

Quitting the Club   *15*
E. LYNN HARRIS

Black Man Standing   *25*
JABARI ASIM

Twisted Street Logic   *41*
BRIAN GILMORE

The Race Industry, Brutality, and the
Law of Mothers   *53*
DAVID DANTE TROUTT

The Black Belt: How Justice Begins at Home   *69*
FRED MCKISSACK JR.

Fear of a Blue Uniform   *81*
RM JOHNSON

My Flesh and Blood: Black Marks and Stigmata   *93*
RICARDO CORTEZ CRUZ

From Within, From Without   *109*
ANDRE JACKSON

Mediation in Black and White: Unequal Distribution of Empowerment by Police   *125*
CHRISTOPHER COOPER

What I Learned in School   *143*
MAT JOHNSON

Police State of Mind   *153*
ROHAN PRESTON

Contributors   *165*

INTRODUCTION:
TWELVE MOODS FOR JUSTICE

(with apologies to Langston Hughes)

Cultural Exchange

In the course of completing this book, I have on more than one occasion fielded well-intentioned queries regarding the progress of "Twelve Angry Men," although I have never burdened this project with such a broad and inaccurate title. I realize that misperceptions of this sort can be seen as illustrating the extent to which Reginald Rose's play has penetrated American imaginations, but they more likely result from people—of various ethnicities—quickly assuming that any black man's contribution to discussions of justice will inevitably be angry. It's ironic that no matter what subject is being addressed, convenient categorization becomes a trap that we black men must evade if we want to be heard, much less understood. Our fellow citizens' inability (or, in some cases, unwillingness) to recognize our true selves accompanies our struggle across widely disparate contexts. It is as easy to see us as angry as it is to assume that we are criminal-minded. While anger is certainly expressed in these pages, it is merely one of a host of responses, as varied and eloquent as the men who have written them. Like the essays included here, we span the gamut of emotions. I invite anyone who chooses to read these essays to regard them as a form of cultural exchange, the considered offerings of twelve thoughtful men.

Write, Read, Write

I've often thought about the concept of "a jury of one's peers." Although the remarkable phrase doesn't appear in our Constitution, it couldn't be far from what the Framers had in mind when drafting the Sixth Amendment's provision of the right to an impartial jury. That clause, together with the Fourteenth Amendment's guarantee of "equal protection of the law," makes a jury of one's peers a reasonable expectation for Americans awaiting trial.

Most of them, anyway.

The damaging tradition of hopelessly narrow jury pools, excessive peremptory challenges, and the routine, historic exclusion of black men from roles other than defendant has often reduced both "peer" and "impartial" to unfamiliar concepts, fleeting illusions to be pursued but rarely attained. It would not be an exaggeration to characterize our troubled relationship with American jurisprudence as one long peremptory challenge. As long ago as 1829, David Walker dared his fellow Americans to "show me a man of colour, who holds the low office of a Constable, or one who sits in a Juror Box, even on a case of his wretched brethren, throughout this great Republic!"

That idea resonated as I envisioned the project that became this book. If I had the chance, I wondered, what kind of men would I select as members of my jury? Given the ubiquity of death-penalty debates, the enthusiasm with which our president regards capital punishment, and the detailed media illustrations of doomed, dark-skinned convicts, it's hardly a far-fetched conceit to imagine oneself on trial, if not for one's life, then for one's freedom to pursue happiness exempt from the prejudices and misapprehensions that frequently complicate our everyday lives. I asked the contributors assembled here to join this project because they embodied the qualities I would hope to find among the members of that panel on my hypothetical day in court. They are sensitive, intelligent, and rational and, like myself, spend much of their lives writing, reading, and writing.

Later, as the essays started to come in, the idea of a jury began to give way to the image of a cocktail party, a smart conversation unfolding amid music, beauty, and the energy that emerges when brilliant minds engage. Still later, I began to embrace an image set forth by Ricardo Cortez Cruz in his essay, that of "twelve black men sitting down at a table addressing/redressing . . . sharing our beliefs, attitudes, and values." As artists, intellectuals, and professional opinionators, much of what we do can be neatly encapsulated by Ricardo's words: Address and redress. Write, read, write.

Shades of Perspective

These essays help expose two frustratingly durable fallacies: the monolithic black experience and the singular black perspective. Not all of these contributors have been arrested, pulled over, or otherwise harassed by police; not all of us have led squeaky-clean lives. An issue or event, though defined by a single fact or set of circumstances, is bound to yield various facets and conclusions when filtered through our quite different sensibilities. Reflections on the Diallo and Dorismond debacles, for example, range from righteous fury to weary resignation to the defiant faith that truth always seeks and finds the light. Our writing styles are likewise diverse. Consider the muscular candor of Mark Anthony Neal's "Just Another 'Nigga,' " the hip-bop hybridity of Ricardo Cortez Cruz's "My Flesh and Blood," the earnest self-scrutiny in Andre Jackson's "From Within, From Without."

Ode to Dissent

We can agree to disagree. We're not seeking consensus here. To paraphrase Lerone Bennett Jr., it's not important that all black people do the same thing; it's more important that all black people do some thing. Ditto for thinking. We humbly propose that the thoughts assembled here be entered into the public conversation, even in those forums where black thinking is summarily dismissed in favor of the arrogant utterings of would-be wise men whose attempts at profundity reveal only the depths of their ignorance. In some quarters, pervasive distrust and hatred of police leads to values so inverted that outlaws become folk heroes—a form of thinking that can lead to deadly consequences for cops and the citizens they have sworn to protect. In "Twisted Street Logic" Brian Gilmore lays out the ramifications.

Blues in Stereo

As compelling as our contentious relationship with law enforcement is, it is not our only problem. We are far more likely to be harmed or killed by another black man than to be brought down by a policeman's bullet. The fact that death by either means is not an entirely improbable occurrence provokes serious discussion and serves up a double dose of the blues. I think it's safe to say that none of these contributors is obsessed with death, harassment, or brutality. Nor do we choose to live as if constantly framed in the crosshairs of an unseen assassin. We are all primarily concerned with living, and to a lesser extent, keen to examine the impact of law and its traditionally uneven application to our lives. Hence, some of these essays hardly mention the police at all. Take, for instance, "What I Learned in School," in which Mat Johnson recalls how his introduction to the codes of the playground helped him adapt to the laws of the street.

Horns of a Dilemma

We are aware of national polls suggesting that the majority of blacks favor harsher treatment of criminals, welcome increased policing, and support construction of more prisons. Those same polls, however, indicate that up to three-fourths of black Americans also believe that the criminal justice system is racially biased and that the majority of policemen are corrupt. Outside academia, the effect of poor policing on the quality of life of those most in need of proficient law enforcement is a problem that has yet to be sufficiently addressed.

Is there any way to alleviate the tension between blacks' definite need for more policing with our defensibly entrenched distrust of cops? RM Johnson takes this dilemma by the horns in "Fear of a Blue Uniform." Christopher Cooper, himself a former cop, examines ways police departments can help citizens solve their own problems in "Mediation in Black and White."

Gospel Truths

"Injustice anywhere is a threat to justice everywhere."
—*Martin Luther King Jr.*

Our concerns go far beyond the university campuses, newsrooms, libraries, and creative laboratories where many of us practice our professions. We realize that "injustice anywhere" too often means "anywhere black men happen to be."

For example:

On the road

On April 23, 1998, New Jersey state troopers stopped four young men—three African-Americans and one Hispanic—driving a van to a basketball clinic in North Carolina. While the troopers investigated the men for possible connections to drug trafficking, the van began rolling backward. The troopers fired eleven shots, wounding three of the men. The two officers involved in the turnpike shooting were subsequently indicted for falsely listing black motorists as white in their reports, deeds that became central facts in New Jersey's ongoing racial-profiling scandal.

In an operating room

At St. Thomas Hospital in Nashville, Tennessee, a black male technician was asked to leave his post at the heart-lung machine at the request of a patient's husband, who did not want "black men looking at his wife's nude body" while she underwent open-heart surgery. Dr. Michael R. Petracek, the surgeon who asked the technician to leave, admitted later that he made "a bad mistake."

At home

On October 4, 2000, police gunned down retiree John Adams after breaking into his Lebanon, Tennessee, home during a botched drug raid. Adams, sixty-four, died protecting his wife, whom police had pushed against a wall and handcuffed after bursting in. The white policemen had knocked down the wrong door, despite the fact that there are only two houses on the entire block. Lebanon police chief Bill Weeks, defending his officers' good intentions, said Adams's death resulted from an "awful and terrible screw-up on our part."

Obviously, not all of our experiences end in death or injury. In the case of the medical technician—and in the cases of men routinely stopped and frisked—inconvenience and humiliation are the prices paid for others' "terrible screw-ups" and "bad mistakes." It is through the accumulation of such inconveniences, however, that injustices emerge. Over time, awareness of the fragility of our right of free passage becomes embedded in our consciousness, innate and readily acknowledged as a gospel truth. As Paul Robeson noted in *Here I Stand,* "From the days of chattel slavery until today, the concept of travel has been inseparably linked in the minds of our people with the concept of freedom." While we fervently wish that the examination of our gospel truths (self-evident, if you will) would lead to justice, all too frequently they lead only to more questions.

How many stop-and-frisks should an individual have to endure before he can credibly cite his experience as an example of injustice? The Fourth Amendment supposedly provides protection against unreasonable searches and seizures, although it did little to help John Adams, the basketball players in New Jersey, or the countless others who have testified to their harassment at the hands of law enforcement. The Supreme Court seems to be oblivious to our testimony. In *Whren v. U.S., Ohio v. Robinette, Maryland v. Wilson,* and other decisions, the Court has continued to expand the right of the police to bypass the Fourth Amendment. Those lamentable decisions in turn expand the necessity for black men to develop an outlook that will enable us to travel across our nation's purple mountains, fruited plains, and dangerous turnpikes with our lives and our dignity intact. Addressing that outlook, Rohan Preston relates his own efforts at self-preservation in "Police State of Mind."

Voir Dire

About seven years ago, I entered an office building in search of a local arts council. I can't remember the exact room number of the council, so let's call it Room 103. I asked the receptionist on duty to direct me to the room. A young black woman with a pleasant disposition, she informed me that I meant to say Room 301. I apologized, followed the directions she gave me, and soon wound up at the entrance to an office where parolees could meet with their probation officers. Instead of being offended I was amused that anyone could mistake such an obvious nerd for a man who had done time. When I related the incident to my wife, she reminded me that many of the black men who passed by the receptionist's station each day probably were indeed on their way to the probation office. Hence the receptionist's mistake was well intentioned, and in fact caused me no embarrassment.

The experience returned to mind while I was reading *The Color of Crime,* a fine study by Katheryn K. Russell. Among her many salient points is the observation that "the onslaught of criminal images of Black men . . . causes many of us to incorrectly conclude that most Black men are criminals. This is the myth of the criminalblackman." The pervasiveness of this myth and its almost immeasurable destructive power influences the daily interactions of even the least paranoid black men. As Russell puts it, "We can only speculate as to the toll—spiritual, psychological, and physical—exacted upon a group whose freedom of movement is consistently challenged." My own essay, "Black Man Standing," tries to provide some measure of this toll. In it, I attempt to speak truly about the complications that arise when the myth of the criminalblackman prevents those charged with protecting us from distinguishing between predators and those law-abiding citizens upon whom they prey.

Mother to Son (Ask Your Mama)

Black men's education regarding life, law, and justice usually begins in the home and, for various reasons, it is often our mothers who begin the socialization process. Maternal wisdom is frequently invoked in these essays, such as Christopher Cooper's recollection that his mother "always told me that because I was black, I could not do some of the things that are legal even though white people do them, because if I do those same things, I will be treated as if I have done something illegal." Similarly, in "The Black Belt," Fred McKissack Jr. remembers that his mother taught him "to tell the truth and shame the devil." With passionate logic (logical passion?) David Dante Troutt outlines the instructive role of the maternal narrative in "The Race Industry, Brutality, and the Law of Mothers."

Words in Orbit

We black American men are among the most misunderstood citizens of this vast and perplexing republic. Many things sustain us: our women, each other, our faith, our labor, and, not least, our words. To borrow from Jean Toomer, we have been shaping words to fit our souls. Words are what we offer here: both for our own enlightenment and in the hope that this time our language will reach beyond our own communities and touch others who might otherwise be disposed to challenge us peremptorily, to dismiss us without cause.

Voices Muted

Amid the neurotic obsession with black men's rage and our alleged propensity to destruction, the effects of our silence are nearly overlooked. What happens to black men and those who love them when our experiences so overwhelm us that we choose not to speak? In his essay, E. Lynn Harris recalls a painful experience during his adolescence, when circumstances willed him to silence. "Since I assumed my fate had already been determined, I decided I would suffer my humiliation alone," he writes in "Quitting the Club."

Show Fairness

The American negro, child of the culture that crushes him, wants to be free in a way that white men are free. For him to wish otherwise would be unnatural, unthinkable.

—*Richard Wright*

Finally, these essays illustrate the degree to which black men's lives are complicated by a sporadic acquaintance with fairness. That so-called level playing field, much discussed and denigrated in some quarters, remains rife with bumps, potholes, and other hazards—in workplaces, on highways, in certain Southern voting booths. Negotiating our way around insidious obstacles, we look in vain for evidence of fairness while fending off accusations of victimology, laziness, inferiority. Thoreau was right when he wrote that "[t]he law will never make men free; it is men who must make the law free." With sweat, tears, and sometimes blood, we black men are doing our part.

Recognition of our entitlement to meaningful citizenship does not require the violation or reduction of anyone else's unalienable rights. It requires only the willingness of our fellow citizens, in the words of Martin Luther King Jr., "to rise up and live the meaning" of this nation's creed, to acknowledge that personal independence—so exalted by this nation's founders—is difficult to attain and enjoy while struggling beneath the weight of permanent suspicion.

Freedom to conduct ourselves with the exuberant abandon that is uniquely American. Freedom to move unmolested. Freedom to go our own way. Freedom to mind our own business. In light of our forebears' epic and bloody struggle for the most fundamental provisions of fairness, it is ironic that some freedoms—long taken for granted by others—remain tantalizingly near, but still out of reach.

—*Jabari Asim*

JUST ANOTHER "NIGGA"

Reflections on Black Masculinity and

Middle-Class Identity

MARK ANTHONY NEAL

I can see it in their eyes:
"who is this nigga boy?"

"shouldn't he be on the chain gang?
hasn't Kmart any openings?
has he escaped from the facility at Collins?
didn't he used to play for our high school team?
it's such a shame that those niggas don't finish school . . .
I wonder if he has a birth certificate . . .
wonder where his green card is . . .
he's probably on welfare . . .
those lazy niggas . . ."

And the friendly ones will say:

"Finishing Up Your Homework?"
"Got a Test Tomorrow?"

"I took a couple of classes at the college. You can get through it,
and be a fine example to your race.
You colored people have come so far . . ."

And I pause quietly,
setting aside my Cafe Latte,
placing the keys of my Acura Integra on the table,
turning off my 486 laptop computer with fax-modem.

I pause quietly
and state,

I do not take exams, I give them,
I do not do homework, I correct it.

I have read more books than you have read in your life.
I will write more books than you will read for the rest of your life.
I may already have more degrees than your immediate family
and receive another one before you contemplate such a feat,

and while this may be all well and good
because it's all good
I do have the sense to realize,
sitting here with my Cafe Latte,
and the keys to my electric blue Acura Integra,
and my 486 laptop computer with fax-modem,
I do realize
that I am still just a nigga boy.

It was during our usual scan of the ten P.M. news on WPIX Channel
11 in New York City that we were first made aware of the shooting of
Amadou Diallo. As former New Yorkers exiled in Schenectady, the
PWT (poor white trash) capital of New York State, watching the ten
o'clock news in New York City is a welcome reprieve to the surreal

"kitty up a tree . . . crack mom with cleaver to blame" stories that seem to dominate our local newscasts. It's also an attempt on our part to remain connected to the city of our birth and the place where our parents still hold out for some far-off, never-to-be-realized better times. The downside is that the daily sound bites from the city's mayor, easily the most enigmatic politician alive, never fail to raise my ire. Recently, after hearing Mayor Giuliani deflect charges that he was insensitive to the travails of Lower East Side residents whose public housing project was being overrun by rodents the size of small cats, my wife suggested that a few folks should organize and bum-rush the mayor's next press conference wearing some of those "Fuck Giuliani" T-shirts we peeped at the Harlem Book Fair and perhaps a box full of the best specimens that could be culled from "Rat City." It was that same kind of insensitivity that angered me in the aftermath of Diallo's shooting and the subsequent shooting of Patrick Dorismond, following which Giuliani had the gall to make public the latter's sealed juvenile record. Though my childhood days spent walking the streets of the place we affectionately call the "Boogie-down Bronx" made me all too familiar with the type of vestibule in which Diallo was murdered, the middle-class lifestyles that our parents tried to prepare us for and that we continue to crave with a vengeance created a necessary distance from the tragedy. From our middle-class perches, it was simply easier to "hate" on Giuliani than to really deal with the implications that another human was the victim of overzealous and perhaps even racist law-enforcement officers.

I've spent a large portion of my professional life in front of college and university classrooms detailing the atrocities imposed on black folks by law-enforcement agencies such as the FBI, the New York Police Department (NYPD), and the Chicago Police Department (CPD). In my mind, a figure like youthful Black Panther Fred Hampton, who was murdered by the CPD in 1969 in what poet Haki Madhubuti has described as a "one-sided shootout," deserves patron saint status within the black community. Attempting to relate to the current crisis of police brutality and its various incarnations, I found comfort in my book contracts, new home, and doting baby daughter. Realistically, what was the likelihood that I would ever be in the position that Diallo was in that night in the Bronx?

My ambivalence remained with me even as the trial of the four officers accused of murdering Diallo was relocated to the city of Albany (a pro-law-enforcement locale), where I currently teach classes at the state university. While a unique blend of feminist, transgendered, and lesbian activists, including the black feminist icon Barbara Smith, emerged from the shadows of the largely stagnant black activist community in Albany to organize daily protest and rallies in front of the courthouse, I was engulfed in departmental battles, publishing deadlines, committee meetings, and the usual assortment of "scholarly" tasks that make real academic activism, like that practiced by my man Robin Kelley or Joy James, a rarity. Hell, I had no problem teaching Barbara Smith's work, something not usually associated with black male scholars within the domain of African-American studies, but when she and others made a call to action, I found solace in the political theories and not the commonsense practice of those ideas. My inability to become fully engaged with the efforts of local activists became my dirty little secret, as my thoughts about the murder, the trial itself, and the subsequent acquittal of the four officers who killed Diallo receded to the margins of my conscience. This was not simple apathy, but rather the product of the realization that even with my newfound middle-class status, I could still experience the terror that Diallo no doubt experienced in that vestibule. I remember admitting as much to my wife, again during the ten o'clock news, after the top four stories one night dealt with the shootings of Diallo and Dorismond, Puff Daddy's legal hassles (largely self-inflicted, I might add), and the sudden but not so surprising death of four-hundred-pound hip-hop artist Christopher "Big Pun" Rios. It seemed as though the newscasters were more or less admitting that black and Latino men were under siege. And while my views as a black male feminist often led me to eschew the type of "let's save the black man" rhetoric that can be found in virtually every black periodical or listserve—because of the powerful ways that they obscure the equally profound crises experienced by black women and others—I guess I was forced to admit that I was scared. Several months after the four officers accused of Diallo's murder were acquitted, I sat in an upscale restaurant in New York City, with my tightest crew of "niggas." I had driven to New York with my daughter, to meet my wife who was there on a business trip. I was able to arrange a chance dinner with my boys, whose own professional demands—one's a New York power lawyer, another a journalist, and the third a college recruiter—often keep us from ever hanging the way we wish we could. On the drive down from Schenectady, I remember how cautious I was to drive the speed limit, so as not to attract any law-enforcement officers. I have become particularly sensitive in this regard since the birth of my daughter, fearing that an inevitable confrontation with law enforcement would leave me unable to tend to her needs. Whereas my Bronx swagger was once an emblem of pride (Uptown, Baby!), I now keep it in check, particularly when it can bring attention from those I am ostensibly powerless to resist. Despite our urgings that we eat dinner at BBQ, a local chain of Texas-style barbecue restaurants, where corn bread, BBQ chicken, and Idaho potatoes can be had for less than six dollars, Gopal, the lawyer and vegetarian, had designs on B. Smith's Restaurant, owned and named after the Afro-Nubian counterpart to Martha Stewart.

While the not-yet-married and childless Gopal fielded queries from his ever-ringing cell phone and deflected charges from us that he could possibly be just a tad bit too "bourgic" for us, Frank, Sebastian, and I exchanged battle stories about day care, the economic challenges of dressing our children in the standards that our wives desire, and our real fear of not being able to protect our daughters and sons from psychic, educational, and physical violence. Though we never once mentioned the Diallo shooting or verdict, the case was a clear subtext to our collective worries about the safety and protection of our families. Like the black jurors who helped acquit the four accused officers, jurors who were described by local commentators in Albany as "responsible" alternatives to the black jurors who acquitted O. J. Simpson, our combined eight college degrees and reasonably comfortable middle-class status (Sebastian, the most "ghetto fab" of our group, has even taken up golf) suggested that we too were "responsible" black folks who supposedly could tell the difference between an accident and acts of racial profiling. This was apparently lost on our waiter who, in response to our desires to pass up alcoholic beverages, apparently viewed us thirty-something black men as potential cheap-ass, tip-stealing, "big Willie" wannabes. It was a subtle reminder that as black men, once we are rendered as symbols of scorn, disparagement, and fear, we can often face abuse from those who ostensibly look exactly like us and are often themselves subject to the same kinds of abuses.

Whatever claims we can make in relation to our economic status—and to be honest, in my case there aren't many past a mortgage, digital TV, a stunning music collection, and the comfort derived from the fact that I am one of those "Niggas with a Ph.D." that Malcolm derided before his death—that status has rarely protected us from the everyday annoyances associated with our race and gender. Perhaps buoyed by DMX's anthem of "ghetto-fab" psychosis "Party Up" ("Y'all gon make me lose my mind up in here . . . up in here"), I once suggested in a classroom discussion about race that I had really come to the point where I wanted to have a reason to kick any "young white boy's ass" for their repeated failure to treat me with the respect that I think my age (I'm thirty-five), economic status, and educational attainment deserve. Most likely the kid serving me at Boston Market, Mickey D's, or Starbucks (my home away from home) is a college student trying to make ends meet, who has no reason to suspect that I'm any different from the black men he regularly sees on the local news. I also realize that we live in a society that is fundamentally rude. I have often wanted to get "Chris Rock" on folks in the supermarket, who regularly remark that my two-year-old daughter was exceptionally well mannered ("how the fuck do you expect her to act . . . be swinging down the breakfast aisle coo-coo for Cocoa Puffs?"). My daughter has developed certain desirable social skills because she has been in day care since she was eight weeks old, though that has not kept her from saying no! to her parents, heresy for those familiar with the tradition of black parenting. As someone who is paid to think, I'm expected to be above such reactionary responses because I know that folks who work in the service sector are underpaid and exploited and often deal with those facts by taking it out on the people they perceive as being in the least position to read them on their trifling attitudes. At a Starbucks in New York City a few years ago, a young white guy gave my wife and me free lattes because he was "sick of white folks," meaning that in an upscale coffee shop heavily populated with white customers and largely absent of black workers (excepting the porters in the back), he had become an "honorary" nigga. The bottom line is that everybody, regardless of their race, ethnicity, gender, social status, etc., should be treated with a common respect, but in a society where we know that has never been the case, we want to share in the idea that these markers of middle-class identity will at least provide us with a reprieve from these annoyances—and they are just that, annoyances. What we tend to find most offensive, given the heavy rhetoric within "Black" America about the value of educational attainment in relation to economic status, are the times when that middle-class status does nothing to protect us from racial profiling, police brutality, and the affliction known as "shopping while black." Though I was raised as a child in a solidly working-class environment (my father was a short-order cook and my mother a school lunch worker), I had my share of glimpses of (faux) black middle-class life via the yearly church outings to Peg Leg Bates's summer resort (thankfully, minus any paper-bag tests) and listening to my mother talk endlessly on the phone about cotillions (the pre–ghetto fab coming-out party). Even then I think I understood that these were attempts, no matter how superficial, by some elements of the black community to experience some semblance of autonomy, particularly for those folks who were not likely to sacrifice their nine-to-fives for a frontline position next to Angela, Huey, or Stokely, and the rest of the "revolution." The fact that my mother often paraded me along instead of my father (he was too country) was a subtle reminder that she was not going to allow me to be like him. She often stated this plainly about four or fives times a week. My mother financed her mid-dle-class sensibilities with an assortment of thirty or more credit cards that kept me thinking that I was indeed middle class even as we "moved on up" to the Pjs. Since that proverbial moment called inte-gration made some black institutions irrelevant, some elements of the black middle class have had to create other mechanisms to derive the power that was derived in earlier years via groups such as Jack and Jill and the assortment of fraternities and sororities that validated black middle-class status. While these organizations still exist and are damn sure still elitist, many of us in the nouveau black middle class (mean-ing we are still a paycheck or two away from poverty) have had to find other ways to articulate our status and revel in our self-deluded notions of importance. Clearly even the crass materialism that seems to afflict many black youth—nothing like an eleven-year-old suggesting that you don't really matter unless you got some "ice"—is a key component of some black middle-class identities. A case in point is the satisfaction that my wife and I get pushing our daughter around in her Peg Perego stroller. The stroller was a gift from my mother and no doubt a prod-uct of her vanity. We protested bitterly when she first shared with us the cost of the gift, figuring that some of that money could have been better spent on more relevant things like say, um, DIAPERS and BABY WIPES. Unbeknownst to us at the time, Peg Perego is the "in" designer baby stroller of the moment, a fact that was later confirmed to us in Al Roker's book on parenting and during an outing to the Bronx Zoo, where passersby mumbled things like "Yeah, that's the one I really wanted." All we knew beforehand was that the shit seemed to ride like a toddler's Volvo. Now we know why. Knowing the status that it appar-ently conveys, we continue to pull the thing out of the trunk of our ten-year-old Honda Accord, despite the fact that my daughter hates being in it.

Even more important than the attainment of material goods, which many of us can't really afford, is the social utility of the act of shopping. I remember a colleague of mine once suggesting that he needed a "mental health day," meaning he could get his spirit back, siphoned away teaching at a historically black college, ironically, by spending some money in an upscale mall in downtown New Orleans. While some of us are severely limited in the amounts that we can actually spend, there is some social "value" in the perception that we can spend in upscale settings and this is often serious business. I understand that many aspects of the middle-class "dream" are simply bankrupt—I don't have any more money to spend now than when I was a struggling grad student, just more money to pay for the larger number of bills. But the moments in which I'm allowed to believe that my middle-class status does matter, like midafternoons at Starbucks sipping Earl Grey and reading Paul Gilroy or purposely writing checks at our local Borders just so "whoever" can read the Ph.D. credentials that follow my name on the checks, often represent psychic retreats from the reality that I am just another nigga.

While I'm cognizant of the superficiality of those times when I'm allowed to be the "special Negro" on the scene, such occasions also become opportunities to engage in the kind of mental play that is sometimes as satisfying as legitimately being able to spend money that I don't have. Even as a youth I got off on these games. I remember once catching a security guard (black, of course) trying to keep tabs on me by following me around an East Side Gristede's and purposely waiting for him as he turned the corner to the aisle I was in to let "bruh" know what was up. As a college student I regularly challenged managers at various stores for their policy of making me check my Swiss-army bag on the premise that since my bag contained my wallet, checkbook, etc., I should be afforded the same courtesy that women with pocketbooks are regularly extended without question. It often got to the point that my boys didn't want to shop with me, but even before the degrees and my now-nuanced intellectual sensibilities, I was always hypersensitive to the proclivity of people to regard young black men as mentally and criminally challenged. Ultimately such attempts at play do little if anything to alter store policies as they relate to who is perceived as potential shoplifters. If anything my legitimate ability to patronize some upscale shops have made me even more of an object of suspicion, because quite frankly, for many people, black middle-class folks don't exist unless they have mad flow, exchange in street pharmaceuticals, or can break a "nigga's" ankle off. This was made powerfully apparent by the choking death of a black man at the hands of a black security guard in the Fairlane Town Center, an upscale shopping mall located in Dearborn, Michigan.

On June 22, 2000, Frederick Finley shopped with his wife, step-daughter, and niece at the Fairlane Town Center. According to police reports, surveillance cameras in Lord & Taylor caught the quartet shoplifting merchandise, including a four-dollar bracelet. As Finley and his family left the store, security officers approached his wife and asserted that her daughter and niece, suspected of shoplifting a four-dollar trinket, had to be detained. A confrontation ensued between Finley's wife and a female security officer. Finley, who had been walking ahead of his family, got involved in the scuffle initially in an effort to protect his family from what he legitimately perceived as an attack. As Finley became more enraged, several security officers, including a black security guard named Dennis Richardson, who held Finley in a chokehold, restrained him. In the ensuing struggle, Finley was choked to death.[1] In the aftermath, some black residents of the city of Detroit and its suburbs suggested that Finley's death was further validation of their previous claims that blacks had been, at best, unwelcome at the mall and, at worst, singled out as potential shoplifters from the time they entered stores such as Lord & Taylor. As protesters held rallies in support of Finley's family, and to bring more attention to Finley's death, one local resident was quoted as saying, "If I'm spending my money, I especially want to be respected. . . . My money is just as green as white people's." The woman's comments were a not-so-subtle reminder that the economic status of blacks often has little to do with how they are treated by certain department-store chains. This idea was further reinforced when Lord & Taylor initially refused to apologize or

---

[1] "Chronology of Fairlane Death," *Detroit News*, 9 Sept. 2000.

send condolences to Finley's family and local prosecutors were slug-gish in charging Richardson with involuntary manslaughter. Finley's death was obscured by insinuations that his death could not be evidence of racial profiling because the guards who restrained him were black. The reality is that those black security guards simply work as agents of a corporate institution that has a vested and legitimate interest in protecting its property. When black guards who are responsible for unfairly targeting black customers as potential shoplifters do so, it is still a form of racial profiling. Finley's death was further shrouded when it was suggested that he and his family were, in fact, shoplifting. Even if this was the case, and all evidence thus far suggests that it was, I cannot ever imagine or accept a context in which someone dies for a four-dollar bracelet.

It was the four-dollar bracelet that perhaps most disturbed me about Finley's death. Like most kids, my daughter, who at two is already a budding feminist and postmodern critic, often has a singular vision in regard to her wants and needs. My wife and I rarely have a problem dealing with her needs; it is her wants that often pose problems, especially during those all-too-frequent Saturday outings to the mall. There is simply no explaining to our toddler that the stuffed animal of which she is currently in possession (conveniently left within her reach by store managers, no doubt hoping that when one is faced with such a dilemma, one will buy said stuffed animal) is going to stay in the store. On one occasion I literally had to negotiate with my daughter—as black parents we cannot allow public tantrums and we have yet to develop that "look" that our own parents gave us when we acted out in public—to get her to accept that the smaller *Blue's Clues* toy was a better choice than the twice-as-large and twice-as-expensive one. Reluctantly buying it for her, I loudly complained about store policies that dictate that things like toys be stocked within the reach of small kids who only seem to understand the word *mine*. My daughter's dexterity at getting her way in department stores inevitably means that one day she will slip one of those four-dollar bracelets on her own wrist and we will unwittingly shepherd her out of the store with stolen goods. While some folks may question our parenting skills—our parents do on a regular basis ("When you were her age you never talked back")—the fact of the matter is that I should not have to be subject to physical violence in the event that my daughter accidentally walks out the store with something that I could have otherwise paid for without blinking. In this regard, Finley's death is even more absurd and surreal than Diallo's. Faced with Finley's dilemma of either protecting his child or allowing her to be subjected to the type of humiliation that African-American adults are regularly forced to accept, I, like Finley, would choose to protect my family.

A few years ago when I was a graduate student, my wife and I lived and worked in a small college town in western New York State. As one of two or three black families who lived in the town, we were often subjected to the weird looks and ignorant comments and questions that inevitably accompany the experience of being "different." It was while sitting in a local coffee shop, fittingly named Upper Crust, that an older white man approached me, my laptop, my stack of books, and my nearly completed dissertation and suggested that I should have done my "homework" last night. He did this on two separate occasions, in the process helping to inspire the poem that appears at the beginning of this essay. As a young African-American man, who was a highly visible campus agitator and adjunct instructor, who happened to be adept at sharing my feelings on race in print, I could afford to write off the experience with a poem. While I can admit now that I was, quite frankly, often an ass, I was somehow protected in this community because as a literate and articulate black man ("oh, you speak so well!"), there were those who were fearful that I would talk loudly and badly about them. This was a strategy that I had learned effectively from the likes of folks such as Al Sharpton and Khalid Muhammad. It was a strategy that Diallo, Dorismond, and perhaps even Finley never had the chance to use and yes, it has allowed me some ability to buffer myself from the everyday nuisances that black folks face. But as my poem suggests, when we are cramped into small spaces, be they vestibules or elevators, we are simply rendered as "niggas." This fact alone means that despite my middle-class status, I must continue to see acts of police brutality and racial profiling as a threat to my own and my family's safety and identity. In that regard part of my own spirit was damaged by the deaths of Diallo, Dorismond, Finley, and the countless other black folks who have and will be harmed at the hands of law-enforcement agencies out of control. Included among those many is Cherae Williams. On September 28, 1999, the thirty-seven-year-old Bronx woman requested police intervention while being physically attacked by her boyfriend. When the officers who arrived failed to respond to her complaint, Williams requested their names and shield numbers. In an act that really highlights the ways in which black male violence against black women often inhabits the same sphere as police brutality, the officers removed Williams from her home, drove her to an empty lot, and proceeded to beat her brutally, breaking her nose and jaw.[2] If we are to be serious about the threats to the lives of black women and men, we must not only hold law-enforcement agencies accountable but also demand that black men stop engaging in activities that endanger themselves and their families, such as drug addiction, alcoholism, sexual violence, homophobia, misogyny, and even patriarchy. It is the least we should do to honor those who have died as just another "nigga."

---

[2] "Officers Accused of Beating Woman," *New York Daily News*, 2 Mar. 2000.

QUITTING THE CLUB

E. LYNN HARRIS

I must admit that I have been a card-carrying member of the please-don't-let-them-be-black club. When something of a tragic nature flashes across the television screen or over the Internet, I say a silent prayer that the perpetrator isn't a person of color. It's not that I am unconcerned if the people involved aren't African-American, but I know when something horrible happens, I will probably be judged by strangers as though I am somehow related to the persons involved. It doesn't matter if the accused is a black man darker than coal or green-eyed with skin the color of the sun.

I got that membership feeling when Rodney King was beaten and after the trial. I felt it when Susan Smith told the nation that her children had been kidnapped by a black man. I felt it when O. J. Simpson was arrested and when he was set free. I felt it when Diallo was shot in the Bronx and then again when the officers were acquitted for his murder. I felt it when shots rang out at Columbine High School. I can't tell you how relieved I was when I found out the shooters were middle-class white students.

We (black men) are targets when we succeed and when we fail. We look guilty and we seem suspicious. I know it has to do with color and country. The history of both. I am considered by many to be successful. After growing up one paycheck from welfare I find myself deeply entrenched in the middle class. Still I find that the middle class can sometimes be an uncomfortable place. I know it could be gone in a moment's notice. I find that the personal choices I make for myself depend largely on the fact that I am a black man, not that I am middle class. I was born black; I worked hard to become middle class. If you think I am paranoid, consider this recent episode in my attempt to display and enjoy my middle-class status.

The lease on my car had expired and it was time to renew it or try out another car. I realized that despite my earning power and my desire to have a car that equals what I had, I was looking for something a little understated. Why? Because I didn't want to be pulled over or punished for driving while black. I could just imagine a white policeman, or even a black one for that matter, wondering if the car I was driving was stolen.

When I decided on an entry-level luxury Mercedes, my paranoia was confirmed when the white salesman explained to me, "In Illinois we require license plates on the front and back of the car. A lot of people don't do it because it's not attractive. But I suggest you do put them on front and back to avoid any unnecessary attention from the policemen." Did he think he was telling me something new? I started to tell him how I had recently sold my gold Rolex because I thought it brought me the wrong kind of attention. Have you ever counted the number of white men or women wearing Rolexes in first class on any flight? I would venture to guess more than 75 percent.

I've had two dealings with law enforcement. Both were more embarrassing than frightening. The first occurred when I was fourteen, the summer before my sophomore year of high school. I was working at Arkansas Paper Company, my first real job, and after two weeks, I was paid just like a real employee. After cashing my check at the bank, I placed four crisp twenty-dollar bills in my jeans pocket and headed for downtown Little Rock to do some shopping. The first thing I wanted to purchase was a wallet. I had never had a wallet because I had never had any money to put in it.

I entered through the revolving doors of F. W. Woolworth's unaware that someone was watching my every move. I located the aisle where they kept men's wallets and spotted a nice imitation-leather black wallet. I inspected the inside, making sure there was a place to keep paper currency and a place for my work and student identification. I checked the price, and thought $4.99 was a fair price. As I headed toward a cash register admiring my new wallet I realized I would have to break one of my twenties to pay for it. If I did that, I wouldn't be able to show my mother and sister how much money I had made. My first thought was to go home, show them the money, and then return to purchase the wallet. At that moment I noticed that I was virtually alone in the section of the store. Why couldn't I just slip the wallet in the back of my jeans and walk out of the store? I had never stolen anything from a store with the exception of a few grapes from the produce stands at the local Safeway. But everybody did that. I had even seen my beloved grandmother taste a grape without paying for it.

I quickly placed my money in the wallet as if it were already mine and headed toward the revolving doors. As soon as I felt the humid Arkansas heat hit my face, I heard a voice say, "Stop right there, young man." I turned to face a large white man in an ill-fitting suit who quickly reached for my arms and asked, "What do you have in your back pocket?"

"Huh?" I quizzed.

"You heard me. What do you have in your pocket?" he asked as he swirled my skinny body around, reached in my back pocket, and pulled out the wallet.

"You're under arrest," he said as he pulled my hands to my back and handcuffed me. Strangers both black and white were looking at me in disgust as he moved me quickly to the curb and a waiting police car.

Moments later, I arrived at the Little Rock police station and was placed in a holding cell. Nobody spoke to me or asked me if I was afraid. They didn't ask my name or where I lived. I sat on a metal cot with a thin and smelly mattress. After about an hour that seemed like days, I was told I would be transported to Juvenile Hall and that my parents would be notified. All I could think about was the beating I was going to get from my mother and the talk that would occur in my neighborhood, spread by nosy neighbors and church ladies. I knew I was headed to reform school, a place where I heard inmates were forced to pick cotton and beaten daily.

Since I assumed my fate had already been determined, I decided I would suffer my humiliation alone. No one would know the embarrassment I had brought on my family and race. I arrived at Juvenile Hall in the same police car that had transported me from downtown. The huge building with a circular driveway looked both massive and daunting. When I walked through the steel double doors, I suddenly became mute. I was asked my name. I looked straight ahead with my lips closed tightly. I was asked my parents' names and phone number. I lowered my head as tears began to roll down my face. I was no longer thinking about the whipping I was going to get, but what my friends would think, and Mr. Seligman, the president of Arkansas Paper Company, who had hired me because he thought I had potential when I had introduced him at a speech he had given at West Side Junior High. How could you have potential with a criminal record? Would I ever enter the doors of high school, much less college?

The authorities at Juvenile continued their questions. I maintained my silence. When they realized I wasn't going to speak, I was placed in a cell with another metal cot, a face bowl, and toilet. The only opening to the outside world was a small, dusty window, covered by wire mesh. For the next three days, this small space would become my home. And I would remain silent, despite the daily visits from the authorities, the people who delivered my food, and my fellow inmates, who yelled out questions to me when the lights went out. "Hey you over there. What are you in for? Can't you talk?" It was like a scene out of a bad prison movie.

Naturally during those days I worried a lot. I worried about my mom and sisters. What were they thinking? That I had been kid-napped and killed by the still-powerful Klan? Maybe my mom would be so worried that she would forget about the whipping I deserved. Maybe they thought I had run away from home.

As time passed, I became comfortable in my silence. My imagina-tion began to take hold. I pictured how my cell in reform school would look. How I would be forced to pick cotton, something my mother had done everything within her power to prevent me from experiencing. How I would have to protect myself from the streetwise bullies who I had avoided like castor oil in my own neighborhood.

On the evening of my third day, I had another visitor in my cell. She was a petite, black woman, well dressed, with a steel-gray pageboy hairstyle. She looked familiar and reminded me of Shirley Chisholm, the popular New York congresswoman. She said hello. I didn't respond. She asked me to stand up. I did. She circled me like she was inspecting me and placed her narrow, ringed finger against her chin. Then she looked me dead in my eyes and said, "You're Bessie's grand-son, aren't you?" I didn't answer but my facial reaction must have spo-ken for me. I was Bessie Gaines's grandson, and a couple of hours later, Bessie's eldest daughter, my mother, Etta, was at Juvenile Hall to pick me up and take me home.

My mother's initial reaction was that of any mother whose child had been missing for more than three days. She grabbed me and hugged me tightly, and I could have sworn there were tears in her eyes. I returned her hug, and I had never been so happy to see someone in my life. Yet my joy was short-lived when my mother whispered in my ears as she hugged me, "I am going to tear your butt up."

I got the whipping I deserved and told myself I would never put my mother or myself in that position again. I felt a deep sadness when I saw her standing before the director of the Juvenile Hall with her head hung down. I felt even worse when my mother in a whisper of a voice told the director she was a divorced mother trying to raise four kids on the salary of a cafeteria worker. Her body language suggested that she had committed a crime, not me. I felt sorry for my mother and told myself I would never put my mother or myself in a situation where we had to lower our heads in shame.

For the most part I have upheld my promise to myself and my mother. There was an arrest at my fraternity house during my junior year of college, when I forgot to cover a check I had written to the local grocery chain. My mother never found out about this. Writing hot checks was so commonplace that I was arrested, booked, and released within an hour. When I made restitution for the check, charges were quickly dropped. Since those early dealings with law enforcement, I haven't even stolen hotel soap or written a check until I was certain my bank had the money in my account. I drive my friends crazy when I am behind the wheel, because I obey the speed limit. I would never transport drugs or open alcohol. After even one glass of wine, I turn to the designated driver or a cab. Even when I am in New York City amid its millions of jaywalking residents, I don't walk until the light tells me to.

The moral to my story is I learned my lesson, fortunately very early in my life. But did I learn all of the lesson? And if so, why I am still angry? I am angry at the ways in which I have allowed the media and law enforcement to color some feelings that I am embarrassed to acknowledge, guilt-laden emotions regarding the way I feel and think about some of my own people.

When I purchased my new car, I was not only worried about being stopped without cause by law enforcement, but also afraid of being carjacked by a person of color when I wandered back to my home turf to attend church or purchase fried chicken at a soul food restaurant in a black neighborhood.

I am ashamed to admit that I don't think twice about who is parked next to me when I enter the garage of my downtown condo, but when I am in the 'hood, I find myself noticing anyone who comes within a hundred feet of me or my car. I become nervous when someone else walks into the liquor store on the west side of Chicago, fearing I might become an innocent victim in a robbery, but I will shop and hold conversations with total strangers when I visit the wine chalet in my neighborhood. Notice that it's called a liquor store on the west side, a chalet downtown.

It is sad that after hearing Susan Smith's allegations, I wondered why the man who kidnapped her children didn't come from parents who taught him that you don't take things that don't belong to you. Sometimes my membership in the please-don't-let-them-be-black club doesn't mean withholding judgment until all the evidence is in. I had already painted the family tree of a man who didn't even exist.

I am disappointed in myself when I recall agreeing with our much-respected leader, Jessie Jackson Sr., when he acknowledged that he has at times been relieved when he looked around at someone trailing him and realized his pursuers were not young black men. I have felt the same way.

I am embarrassed that I wondered what Rodney King had done to provoke the Los Angeles policemen other than being black. At first, I questioned, if O.J. wasn't guilty, then why did he run? When I heard the initial reports of the shooting up in the Bronx, I was waiting to hear what type of gun they would find in Diallo's pocket after they had subdued this frightening-looking black man. Like some nonmembers of color it didn't cross my mind that this frightened, not frightening, young man didn't fully understand the way he was supposed to react when men who weren't dressed like law-enforcement officers barked commands at him. He was, after all, from another country. A country where people looked like him and spoke his language.

I am most angry that my newfound middle-class status has damaged my sensitivity toward members of my own race. So many times I assume, like the majority race, that men of color (especially young ones) look guilty and seem suspicious.

On a recent book tour, I was in downtown Seattle taking a break and enjoying the city, a breathtakingly beautiful town where the media had led me to believe the only thing with which I had to concern myself was rain. I was walking down a busy street when I noticed a group (my initial reaction was pack) of young black men heading in my direction. They were dressed in hip-hop regulation clothing, baggy shirts, jeans hanging below the butt, imitation jewelry around their necks and in their ears, and of course their voices were booming. I immediately looked in another direction. I even pretended to be window-shopping rather than make eye contact with my young brothers. While standing there waiting for them to move on, I could feel a pair of eyes looking at me from the window's reflection. I began to feel uneasy, knowing the last thing I was looking for was a confrontation with young men who might be carrying weapons in their book bags. When the young man's look became a stare, I decided to move on and just take my chances. When I turned, I was face-to-face with a tall and lanky young man. Suddenly his eyes didn't look scary. He looked at me and in a voice that reminded me of my favorite teenage nephew asked, "Are you E. Lynn Harris?"

"Yes," I replied, shocked that this young man would know who I was.

"For real? I've read all your books," he said. It appeared to me that the carriage of his body had changed. He seemed like a normal teenager, someone I had once been. It was not the young man who had changed, but my own defense mechanism, which had slipped away when the young man called my name.

I asked him how old he was and he told me he was sixteen. He was looking at me like I was Tupac Shakur or Puffy Combs, while his other friends had moved on down the block.

"Can I ask you something?"

"Sure."

"Can I shake your hand? Man, you are da bomb," he smiled.

As I shook his hand, I wanted to thank him for the lesson he had taught me, but instead I thanked him for reading my books. As I continued my walk, I became ashamed of the fear I had felt moments before. Ashamed of how I often claimed in public speaking engagements how I want to use my books to dispel stereotypes and myths of certain segments of the population. Myths and stereotypes that I now found myself harboring, under the guise of being middle-class. I was still a black man. A black man who had just learned a valuable lesson from a younger and wiser black man. My hope for him and his friends is now clear. I hope they never encounter people who judge them based on their appearance. I hope they never have any type of negative dealings with a member of law enforcement. I pray they never experience a Rodney King or Amadou Diallo incident, just as I am sure my family prayed I never had to experience a Selma or Birmingham. And I hope they never hold membership in the please-don't-let-them-be-black club. A club to which I have recently submitted my resignation.

BLACK MAN STANDING

JABARI ASIM

Race, Again

Sometimes you want to shout about race from the highest rooftop, mount a soapbox, open a vein. Sometimes you don't. You just want to chill, to hunker down in your cubicle and pretend for a few cherished seconds that race doesn't matter. DuBois didn't know what the hell he was talking about, you want to snicker, there's no such thing as a color line. Soon, regular as clockwork, reality comes crashing in. A female coworker who chatted with you in the elevator fails to recognize you when you share a bench at the Metro stop. Just an hour ago the two of you were discussing the upcoming baseball season; now she's clutching her bag tenaciously and twisting her body so far away from yours it's a wonder her spine doesn't crack. Another colleague is the king of courtesy all afternoon, wondering if you heard him casually refer to a black neighborhood as "Niggertown."

Those are worst-case white-collar scenarios; the best are equally tiresome. As a generally good-natured black man who's comfortable in the company of whites, I have on countless occasions been called upon to perform the role of Explainer. Pretending to summon knowledge from that mythical wellspring of collective racial wisdom, I become an oracle dispensing insightful nuggets about Al Sharpton, Jesse Jackson, Colin Powell, Colin Ferguson, gangsta rap, chitlins, bid whist, and the mechanics of the slam dunk to a grateful audience. It's a lose-lose situation, despite my white friends' best intentions. If I indulge them, my comments may enlarge in importance until they represent the opinions of every black man in America. If I refuse them, my friends may stray off the path to enlightenment and wander into the forest of ignorance—or even worse, they may have to find another black friend.

Writing about race is a similarly thankless task. Often I'm asked to review books that cover racial issues because editors assume that I possess a certain degree of expertise in this area. Whether or not I do isn't of paramount importance here; what matters is I don't disabuse them of this notion. In fact I often volunteer for such duties because, I figure, better me than some knucklehead. And race does happen to be one of those precious few subjects that white editors/writers/thinkers may actually concede I am qualified to address. If it weren't for those assignments, perhaps they wouldn't call me at all. It often comes down to a question of commerce: the editor needs a writer and I need cash. To be fair, on other occasions I have accepted assignments that on the surface have nothing to do with race. However, in the course of completing them I become aware of a subtle shift in the direction of the piece, an inevitable, irresistible inclination toward things racial—despite my best efforts to the contrary. It's the push-pull quality of such issues, that funky conflation of attraction and repulsion—that influenced my decision to assemble these thoughts. I didn't want to write about Amadou Diallo. I have had other opportunities to write about similar cases—all too often!—and have passed. Rodney King and his fiery aftermath came and went without my two cents. Ditto for Abner Louima. Intending to shrug off the obvious ramifications of the Diallo verdict as well, I retreated to my cubicle, determined to let it go.

Except I couldn't.

Always in Season

I am holding in my hands a book called *Without Sanctuary*[1] when a friend phones to tell me the news: All of the defendants in the Amadou Diallo trial have been acquitted. I am neither astonished nor dismayed. As he expresses his displeasure, I'm leafing through page after page of photographs of lynched Americans, not all of them black, not all of them men. While my friend speculates as to the future livelihood of Officers Carroll, McMellon, Boss, and Murphy, my eyes light on a 1909 photo of four white men staring sternly into the camera as they pose before helping to lynch a black man named Will James. "Law enforcement agents and bloodhounds," the caption reads. The irony is not lost on me.

No text is devoted to Will James, so we have no idea what he'd done or allegedly done to arouse the ire of the posse that killed him. There is only a series of photographs: "before" shots of Will, a.k.a. "Froggie," a stout, bullnecked man with a bushy mustache; the proud lawmen who tracked him down; the huge crowd that gathered to watch his execution. These are followed by "after" shots: a group of boys (one of them appears to be black) poking at James's ashes with a stick; his severed, half-burned head mounted on a pole; the citizens of Cairo, Illinois, standing near the spot where his "body was riddled with bullets, after being lynched Nov. 11th '09."

Riddled with bullets.

My friend hangs up. The phone rings again. It's my wife, incensed. I knew this call was coming: We have four sons. For the next ninety minutes she keeps me on the line, swearing, calling on God, weeping her guts out. "What am I supposed to tell them?" she demands. "How can I tell my babies that their lives are worth nothing?" My wife is

---

[1] *Without Sanctuary: Lynching Photography in America*, ed. James Allen (Santa Fe, N.M.: Twin Palms Publishers, 2000).

shrill, hoarse, melodramatic. She careens down dark tunnels of the psyche, scary places I have no interest in exploring. I'm at work after all, pretending to do my job while watching video news footage on the Court TV website. Thank goodness for modern technology.

I see a snapshot of Amadou, one of those images of him we've seen countless times. He appears to be wearing a baseball cap, turned fashionably backward atop his head. A broad, bright smile stretches between his prominent cheekbones. I realize my wife is probably looking at a similar picture. I can hear the newscasters droning in the background. Against my will, I imagine Amadou in his vestibule. Eyes wide in surprise. Fingers curled around his wallet. Riddled with bullets.

Before he can morph into one of my sons, I spin around in my chair.

"Are they there?" I ask. She knows I mean the kids.

"Yes," she replies. "They're right beside me on the couch. Watching."

We've gone over the drill more times than we care to remember. Keep your receipts handy. Refuse to be provoked. Ask for a lawyer right away if they take you in. We're especially concerned about Joe. He's seventeen, 211 pounds, a varsity wrestler feeling his oats. During the week we cut out articles from newspapers and magazines. Sundays we read and discuss them. Articles about successful black men share the spotlight with tales of brothers gone wrong. Soldiers, statesmen, rapists, and thugs parade across our tongues. Our two oldest sons, both teenagers, tend to respond to the most dramatic stories. For instance, an article about police officers arresting an innocent man who happened to have the same name as a wanted criminal drew a spirited reaction, as did Bob Herbert's *New York Times* columns about the dangers of breathing while black.

"Hellhounds," Leon F. Litwack's insightful essay included in *Without Sanctuary*, emphasizes the cheapness of black life during the late nineteenth and early twentieth centuries, during which lynch

mobs killed nearly five thousand blacks. He quotes one black south-
erner who recalls, "In those days it was 'Kill a mule, buy another. Kill a
nigger, hire another.' They had to have a license to kill anything but a
nigger. We was always in season."[2]

The policemen who shot Diallo, however incompetent and misguided, can hardly be confused with a lynch mob. Diallo's death, as
horrifying as it was, lacked the elements of spectacle, ritual, and prior
intent that characterize most lynching parties. To call the young immigrant's nightmarish exit a lynching would both betray his memory and
diminish to absurd proportions the horrors endured by all those who
died by rope, faggot, and mob mania. Still, when Sunday rolls around
and we gather our clippings to discuss the verdict and revisit other
aspects of this tragedy, we have to acknowledge certain parallels. Like
poor Will James and most of the other 4,742 blacks lynched between
1882 and 1968, Amadou was outnumbered, outgunned, and subject to
the irrational will of his pursuers.

My sons and I resemble Diallo about as much as he resembled the
serial rapist his killers were allegedly stalking when they brought him
down. Nonetheless, I've certainly engaged in the behavior that Officer
Carroll has described as suspicious. I've left my home, looked up and
down the street, then gone inside, only to return a few minutes later
and repeat the whole process. I've usually been looking for a taxi that
I've called—although that's really irrelevant because I'm talking about
where I live, and what I do there is nobody's business but my own. It's
a nearly all-white neighborhood, however, white enough to throw a
few astonished and concerned stares my way when I walk down the
street—the same street I've been walking down for nearly four years.
Media reports have contained stories of "tragic misunderstandings"
often enough for me to consider the possibility that some evening in

[2] Leon Litwack, "Hellhounds," quoting from Neil R. McMillen, *Dark Journey:
Black Mississippians in the Age of Jim Crow* (Urbana, Ill.: University of Illinois
Press, 1989), 224.

the thickness of dusk, a nervous homeowner could mistake me for a threat to his safety. The scenario likely lurks in the minds of even the most rational of black men: A shot rings out. He falls. The neighbor, his gun still smoking in his hand, realizes his error. At the trial—if indeed there is one—he'll sob uncontrollably, beg forgiveness from the widow.

In real life, the neighbor peers at me from the shelter of his shrubbery, his odd half-smile illustrating how he balances between mere curiosity and genuine suspicion. Put dramatically, my life hangs in that balance.

"There are people worldwide who are working day and night to stop our future."[3]

Haki Madhubuti was referring to the forces of white supremacy when he wrote those words in 1984. To a group still bearing scars from memorable clashes in Selma, Montgomery, and Little Rock, still reeling from the ravages of COINTELPRO, and still licking the wounds left by a string of assassinations, Madhubuti's warning carried the unmistakable ring of truth. He could have converted any lingering skeptics simply by pointing to lynching's lamentable legacy. Four thousand seven hundred and forty-two futures, stopped dead.

In the days since Madhubuti's observation, however, the forces of white supremacy have undergone cosmetic adjustments. Like David Duke, they've ventured underground and emerged with a brand-new face. And they've replaced their customary rabble-rousing inanities with the subtler jargon of judicial retrenchment and ill-conceived Contracts with America. At times they've even co-opted the terminology of their opponents. For example, in 1995, anti–affirmative action activists in the Golden State called their ballot measure the California Civil Rights Initiative, of all things! As Carol Becker

---

[3] Haki Madhubuti, *Earthquakes and Sunrise Missions* (Chicago: Third World Press, 1984), 175.

would remind us, not even progressive language is safe from appro-
priation.[4] So much for semantics, though. Some of us see little difference between George Wallace standing in a schoolhouse door in
1963, proclaiming his commitment to segregation, and Patrick
Buchanan facing the Republican faithful in 1992, urging them, "Let's
take our culture back, let's take our country back." Similarly, our
knowledge of the long blue line stretching from Sheriff Jim Clark and
Bull Connor to Frank Rizzo and Darryl Gates only serves to reinforce
our widely held notion of cops as willful agents of our destruction.
But that was then. These days, black men's ambitions—and lives—are
often threatened by a predator of a decidedly different color. As Stan-
ley Crouch and others have pointed out, a black man is far more likely
to be harmed by another black man than by a policeman, Southern,
Northern, or otherwise. "In New York," Crouch wrote in a recent
essay in Salon.com, "from 1991 to 1996, 4,840 black people were
murdered by civilians while 82 were killed in police shootings." Five
years. Nearly five thousand futures. Stopped dead. With apologies to
James Byrd Jr., it's no wonder you hardly hear of lynchings anymore.
They are so last century.

Because nearly a third of African-American males between the
ages of twenty and twenty-nine are either imprisoned, on probation, or
on parole, few middle-class blacks are more than a phone call away
from intimate contact with the penal system. Like the ominous statistics in Litwack's essay, our friends' and families' experiences with "justice" only confirm the cheapness of black lives. One relative,
imprisoned for killing a black man, was back on the street in three
years. Another was fingered in the widely reported murder of a white
man. He was sentenced to sixty years. Truth-in-sentencing laws, the
judge told him, eliminate the possibility of parole.

Thanks to diligent parenting, my sons possess a proportionate

---

[4] Carol Becker, "The Artist As Public Intellectual," in *The Politics of Culture*, ed.
Gigi Bradford, Michael Gary, and Glenn Wallach (New York: The New Press,
2000), 236.

view of our condition in these United States. My wife and I have emphasized neither extreme of our history. My sons know that a few African-Americans have descended from kings and queens. They also know that a few of us have descended from folks who sold their own people into bondage. Between those two poles exist the rest of us in large numbers, the mostly invisible, hardworking middle. Decent, ordinary, sincere. My sons know how they must conduct themselves to retain their membership in that glorious center.

Acknowledging their precarious status, we have provided them with a commonsense approach to personal safety that includes avoiding questionable people and staying away from dangerous places. Still, they know that we can't keep them safe once they step outside, that in a world where standing in the doorway of one's home is seen as reasonably constituting suspicious behavior, all bets are off. Like me, they have already digested what Amadou Diallo—through no fault of his own—discovered too late: As black men, we are always in season.

Just Us

The fact that some of us regard ourselves as likely targets of both white venom and black dysfunction doesn't mean that we have succumbed to the narcotizing effects of paranoia. Nor have we embraced the peculiar comforts of victimhood. *Victim* is such a loaded word these days; too often its use connotes an aspect of judgment, a suggestion that the wronged have somehow brought about their own undoing. Even worse is the contention that black victimhood can be used effectively as a lever to gain concessions from whites.

It's true that some blacks have pimped victimhood for all it's worth. Perhaps no one has done so as loudly and egregiously as Al Sharpton. For most of his public career he has epitomized foolishness. The Diallo shooting, however, has shown him in a different light. For the most part he has been calm and determined, shrewdly funneling the fury of his constituents into an organized movement for social change. Whether he continues in this vein or reverts to his old, dreadfully unwise ways remains to be seen. He's an anomaly regardless; the rank and file of black citizens have found little to celebrate or exploit in our centuries-long stint as the principal focus of white America's fits of rage.

Even so, some observers insist on seeing victimhood as a bargaining chip used in negotiations between blacks and whites. Shelby Steele, for instance, describes the two races as competing power groups. To view them as such is to assume—falsely—that both groups have power. Black people don't have power. What we have is moments of influence—windows of opportunity that open and shut at the whim of a mercurial white majority whose motives are often difficult to decipher and whose behavior is even harder to predict. Living in the United States as a frequently despised and distrusted minority is similar to entering an elevator with that ubiquitous white female colleague. Will she smile and say good morning? Or will she clutch her handbag and squeeze herself into the farthest corner? Will she engage or will she exclude? The exhaustive nature of the guessing game just adds more complication to an already complex scenario. Those moments of influence have occurred during critical conjunctions of white self-interest and black pursuit of what the Framers drolly described as inalienable rights. (Or, as in the case of the Civil War, during periods when competing white interest groups reached a state of irreconcilable differences.)

Steele also suggests that the goal of black provocateurs is to put whites in touch with what he calls collective guilt. This is hardly an example of power, except perhaps the power to annoy, the way a fly annoys a horse by staying just out of reach of its tail. If there is indeed such a thing as collective guilt among whites (I, for one, remain unconvinced both of its existence and its necessity. Why should anyone need to feel guilty in order to treat me decently?), one can't help but wonder how it compares when measured against the collective assumption of black guilt that colors many whites' dealings with us. If not for these communal convictions, such crass ploys as George Bush's 1988 invocation of Willie Horton would have failed to touch a responsive chord in white voters.

Obviously New York law-enforcement officials are among those whites who harbor such assumptions. In their view, the thirty-six thousand men who were meaninglessly detained during the Street Crime Unit's reign of error were merely inconvenienced. Over the course of a lifetime, the weight of accumulated inconveniences becomes a form of real power—over us—because unlike, say, the nuisance of being mugged, this particular form of "inconvenience" is carried out by agents of the state. Pestered in a nation that guarantees equal protection under the law, black men find themselves in the unique position of desiring protection *from* the law. Our plight has roots that extend deep into the past. Consider a poster from 1851, which reads in part,

Caution!!
Colored People
Of Boston, One & All
You are hereby respectfully CAUTIONED and
Advised, To Avoid Conversing With The
Watchmen and Police Officers
Of Boston, For Since the Recent ORDER OF THE MAYOR &
ALDERMAN, They are empowered to act as
KIDNAPPERS
AND
Slave Catchers, and they have already been actually employed in
KIDNAPPING, CATCHING, AND KEEPING
SLAVES . . .

"Therefore," the poster goes on to advise, "shun them in every possible manner." This predicament helps to shape our profound ambivalence toward the legal system and influences our behavior in the courts, behind bars, in barbershops and shopping malls, in the studios and nooks where we fashion our art. The latter has afforded an essential forum through which we can safely vent understandable feelings of humiliation, rage, and disgust. Often they are aimed at the most visible agents of the law: policemen. In "Southern Cop," master poet Sterling Brown tells the story of Ty Kendricks, a white rookie policeman who has killed a black man without just cause.

> Let us condone Ty Kendricks
> If we cannot decorate.
> When he found what the Negro was running for,
> It was all too late;
> And all we can say for the Negro is
> It was unfortunate.

N.W.A. famously took up the banner in 1988:

> Fuck tha police
> Comin straight from the underground
> Young nigga got it bad cuz I'm brown
> And not the other color so police think
> They have the authority to kill a minority.

Among African-Americans, one needn't be a poet or rap star to participate in our ongoing conversation about cops, courts, and consequences. Many of my middle-class peers who've never darkened the doorstep of a law school can recite a litany of relevant decisions. *Dred Scott v. Sandford. Plessy v. Ferguson. Brown v. Board of Education.* Our complicated relationship with American justice makes lawyers of us all.

We are, after all, the only Americans who required constitutional amendments merely to exercise the rights and privileges of citizenship with relative impunity. It has been an arduous journey from fractions ("three-fifths of a person") to full-fledged Americans. Despite the Framers' willful ignorance and our subsequent defeats suffered before the benches of recalcitrant jurists, the law has often provided our last, best chance for equality. The NAACP's recognition of this fact led to the emergence of legal warriors such as Thurgood Marshall and his allies, who battled for our rights in the courts while Martin Luther King Jr. and others fought for control of America's conscience. The legalist approach was always tempered by the Christian inclinations of those who led it, namely, faith in the eventual triumph of good over evil. Because of this overriding belief in a higher law, blacks have never really expected litigation to be a panacea for the nation's afflictions, but a stopgap measure to stem the tide until the moral evolution of white American society is complete.

At the heart of this epic struggle lurks a contagious, persistent reluctance on the part of whites to see us as fully human. Recognition of our humanity would, in theory at least, afford us access to the fundamental freedoms that citizenship allegedly provides—inalienable rights, if you will. Freedom from undue harassment. Freedom from stop-and-frisk. Freedom to contemplate the splendors of solitude without being mistaken for a car thief, jewel thief, purse snatcher, dope pusher, or rapist. Freedom from the casual cruelties and random, accumulated inconveniences that slow us down and make a mockery of American claims to fairness and justice. This reluctance is often most harshly felt along the nation's highways and in the corridors and precinct houses of the inner cities, hunting grounds favored by our occupying army, the Slave Catchers of our dreams. Who have been known to subdue us with cattle prods, tie us like hogs, deride us as gorillas in their midst. The myopia that fails to distinguish black men from beasts is a variant of the distorted perception that turns a wallet into a gun.

Tragedies like the shooting of Amadou Diallo have a "profoundly depressing familiarity," the *New York Times* has noted. "A white police officer responds to a call involving a Black or Puerto Rican youth, a shot is fired and the youngster dies. Later, though the stories are confusing, the police officer is said to have thought he saw a lethal weapon—a gun or a knife—in the dead youth's hand. It turns out that the weapon cannot be found or is substantially more innocent than the officer thought it was when he discharged his gun."

The "dead youth" in this instance was fourteen-year-old Claude Reese Jr. The year was 1974.[5] Clearly the Police Athletic League and periodic classroom visits from Officer Friendly have done little to improve relations between African-Americans and the folks we pay to protect us. We may have come a long way from the bloody beatdown at the Edmund Pettus Bridge, but law enforcement's long history of bloodshed and brutality still looms between us and them like a line of cops in riot gear. Grassroots efforts aimed at curbing abusive polic-ing—civilian review panels and the like—tend to falter in the face of union opposition, inadequate funding, and inconsistent community support. On the federal level, with the possible exception of the Justice Department's Community Relations Service (CRS), hand-wringing and buck-passing often substitute for action. According to *Emerge* magazine, countries such as Canada, England, and South Africa are easily outpacing U.S. efforts at police oversight.

When I edited a small community-based magazine in St. Louis during the early '90s, we prepared a special issue focusing on relations between black St. Louisans and the local police force. For one story, a colleague sat in on a sensitivity class that officers were required to take at that time. He watched in horror as the cops joked and whispered and otherwise ignored their instructor until the class was over. My col-league's experience illustrates what all efforts at improving the quality of law enforcement must ultimately confront: the resistance of the offi-cers themselves to overcome their own prejudices and misconcep-tions—most of which were cemented long before they took their oath of service.

If they manage such a transformation, they'll see that my brothers

---

[5] Joseph B. Treaster, "NYC Patrolman Frank Bosco Interviewed on Shooting of 14-year-old Claude Reese in Brownsville," *New York Times*, 21 Sept. 1974.

and I seek no entitlement or special acknowledgment deriving from our previous condition of invisibility; we desire nothing more or less than recognition of ourselves as men, capable of both accomplishment and failure, honor and disgrace. It hardly seems unreasonable to expect our fellow Americans to consider such things when next they chance upon a black man standing—on the corner, in his doorway, on his principles.

"Not once have the Civilized been able to honor, recognize, or describe the Savage," James Baldwin wrote at his ironic best. At the turn of the century, his wisdom still applies.

Raving

Now will the poets sing,—
Their cries go thundering
Like blood and tears
Into the nation's ears,
Like lightning dart
Into the nation's heart.

Countee Cullen

In a poem called "Scottsboro, Too, Is Worth Its Song," Countee Cullen called on his partners in rhyme to use their talents in the service of a cause. The Scottsboro Boys, nine in number, were arrested in 1931 for the rape of two white women. They were tried and convicted in two hours, despite the absence of incriminating evidence. All were sentenced to death but the youngest, who received a life sentence. Most uncharacteristically, Cullen insisted that poets pick up their pens and begin composing protests against this colossal injustice, this "epic wrong." Cullen, who favored traditional European forms in his work and discouraged the earthier experiments of his contemporary Langston Hughes, had long fought against any activist stirrings he may have felt. Having published his first volume in 1925, he was already past his prime by the time of the Scottsboro trial. Ultimately he recognized himself as a poet of paradox, a writer who succeeded best at themes he admired the least. "I find that I am actuated by a strong sense of race consciousness," he admitted. "This grows upon me . . . it colors my writing, I fear, in spite of everything I do."

The conflict to which Cullen alludes—the tension between the specifics of black existence and the "universal" arena in which all human drama unfolds—also is the engine propelling my own anguished scribblings, indeed much of black art. Larry Neal explained this seemingly eternal tug-of-war between the personal and the political as the "two contending trends in Afro-American thought, that is, the will toward self-definition, exclusive of the overall white society, and at the same time the desire not to be counted out of the processes of so-called American democracy." In other words, two warring ideals in one dark body.

In some sense, we writers are all poets of paradox. We demand precious isolation from the world in order to testify of events taking place in its blood-soaked dirt and sticky streets. These words of mine, for instance, were cobbled together in the safe confines of my suburban study. If we're feeling particularly haughty, we can claim to be engaging in a form of organic intellectualism, struggling to change minds and affect lives through the passion of our words. Remembering Baldwin's dictum that man is also "enjoined to conquer the great wilderness of himself," I can for the moment satisfy myself that writing is indeed a form of fighting, that wrestling the chaos within enables me to shine a telling light on the chaos without.

Then again, perhaps it's not as complicated as all that. "We're all ravers, in one fashion or another," Amiri Baraka once noted when he was still LeRoi Jones. Maybe it suffices to say that I hope my ravings—albeit off-key and occasionally discordant—might somehow be taken for music, that reaching across decades and causes, I am answering

Cullen's call. The reasons I sing are simple enough, I think. I sing because each man's death diminishes me. I sing to let off steam. I sing to the memory of a young man from Guinea who voyaged through life to find death upon these shores. I sing knowing that thousands of words may never equal nineteen bullets. I sing because Amadou Diallo, too, is worth his song.

TWISTED STREET LOGIC

BRIAN GILMORE

"Though innocent, he felt guilty, condemned."
—*Richard Wright*

I

February 11, 1980. Bruce Wazon Griffith, a small-time drug dealer in Washington, D.C.'s once infamous Fourteenth Street corridor, shot D.C. metropolitan police officer Arthur Snyder to death after Snyder attempted to arrest him on the street. Griffith, who was black, shot Snyder, who was white, because Snyder was a mean cop and had always brutally harassed Griffith and others in that area. Griffith shot Snyder once in the chest but because Snyder was wearing a vest, the bullet only knocked him down. Griffith then walked up to Snyder while he was on the ground, stood over him, and shot him in the head. I do not know if this is really how it happened, but that is the story that eventually made it to the streets. Four days later in a shoot-out at First and S Streets, N.W., the police shot Griffith to death.

Griffith's legend grew larger in the days and weeks and even years following his violent demise. "Reds," as Griffith was known on the street, supposedly hung out all over the city after killing Snyder, never once hiding from the police. At a downtown bus station, he allegedly bragged that he was Snyder's killer and flashed a roll of bills that he said could take him to freedom. However, Reds stayed in the city, shot it out with the police, and became a folk hero overnight.

Nearly every black male under thirty years of age in my neighborhood, a middle-class African-American uptown neighborhood called Riggs Park, had been rooting for Griffith to escape. As the manhunt pressed forward, and Reds remained at large, many of us hoped he had left the country. I was only seventeen years old at the time and already I despised the police.

Maybe I felt that way because when my friends and I would come home from parties late on Friday or Saturday nights, the local police (both black and white cops) would always seem to be waiting for us right in our neighborhood, giving us dirty looks from their slow-moving squad cars, baiting us into verbal exchanges with them, and sometimes chasing us through the streets for reasons that seem confusing now. Or maybe it was because when we stood on the corners or in the alleys in our neighborhood, the cops felt that it was necessary to threaten us with arrest unless we obeyed their orders to disperse.

Then again, my hatred may have stemmed from the older black men around the way, who I suspected knew the black man's experience with the cops better than I did. They passed along their naked contempt for the police freely, raging at every opportunity about "da pigs." Being very impressionable, I would digest their one-sided views about cops as gospel that I eventually incorporated into my daily life even as I accumulated my own experiences with the police. In light of all of those circumstances, Bruce Wazon Griffith easily grabbed my attention in 1980, as well as that of most of the other young black men in the city.

According to Richard Cohen, writing in the *Washington Post* at the time, four thousand people from all walks of life attended Griffith's wake. Cohen said that Griffith had become a hero due to "twisted street logic." He missed the point.

Griffith more than likely shot Arthur Snyder in cold blood, but that does not change the fact that four thousand people, black people mostly, decided it was important to pass by Griffith's casket. Although he did not commit a political homicide on February 11, 1980, the community tried to transform it into one. Some tried to make it seem as if Griffith's actions were as politically purposeful as those of Nat Turner, even though Griffith's conduct appeared to be almost entirely personal. Such efforts, however misguided, exemplify the frustration some black people occasionally feel and the hidden anger—fueled by oppression, not twisted street logic—that many contend with on a daily basis.

The murder of Officer Snyder happened twenty years ago but the same kind of tragedy occurred again in 1993, when a young white police officer named Jason White was gunned down in D.C. by a young black man named Donzell McCauley. In my neighborhood, I didn't hear one young black man condemn McCauley for his actions. In fact, once rumor spread that McCauley killed Officer White because he had "dissed" McCauley, people started to refer to the young murderer as a "soldier." It was another act of murder in black America suddenly being transformed into something larger because of America's tortured racial history. It's that same tragic, often suppressed history of slavery, segregation, and oppression—again, not twisted street logic—that makes heroes of outlaws and influences black people (at least the black people with whom I interact daily) to distrust white people. This is especially true in the case of authority figures such as law-enforcement officials. These are black people, myself included, who exercise this general distrust even while maintaining individual relationships with whites as friends, coworkers, neighbors, and confidants. If you don't believe this, perhaps you need to inquire sometimes; perhaps someone will speak to you forthrightly.

II

Albert Camus put it best when he said that racism is absurd. It is. I can think of no better word to describe racism's role in the world and American society. Camus's colleague, expatriate African-American

writer Chester Himes, expanded upon Camus's notion: "If one lives in
a country where racism is held valid and practiced in all ways of life,"
Himes once wrote, "eventually, no matter whether one is a racist or a
victim, one comes to feel the absurdity of life." How some black people in Washington, D.C., reacted to the actions of Bruce Wazon Griffith only indicates how absurd American life is and continues to be
under the spell of racial injustice. Black people feel so betrayed at times
by their own country and their fellow citizens that they find themselves rallying around incidents such as Griffith's murder of a white
cop or O. J. Simpson's acquittal. Scrambling to come up with a rationale, they claim these events as victories for the race. Such thinking is
clearly unreasonable but it is directly related to the black experience in
this country. Sadly, we all know that racism and all of its complexities
are still not behind us in America.

Why did all of those law students at Howard University School
of Law leap in the air cheering for a black sports celebrity found not
guilty of killing two white people, a black sports celebrity who rarely
wanted to have anything to do with black people? Why do I watch
Tiger Woods each and every time he plays golf on television and
cheer for him with a passion even though I hate golf and think it is an
elitist sport with an embarrassing racial history? Why did a large portion of the white people living in the nation's capital move out of the
majority-black city after civil rights laws promoting integrated neighborhoods were passed? For that matter, why are most white Americans
still living in segregated neighborhoods, attending segregated schools,
worshiping in segregated churches apart from their black country-
men? Not to say that "integration" should be the primary goal of black
people, but the list of pertinent questions on race issues is, perhaps,
endless.

Not long ago, when I arrived to park in one of Washington's downtown lots, the attendant scrutinized my parking pass as if he were a sci-
entist looking for an unknown virus under a microscope. At the same
time, whites parked their cars and waved their passes at him from afar.

I came out of an uptown bookstore one night in the city recently and passed close to a white woman's car. She locked her doors just as I got close. I laughed as I started up my own car and thought that she probably didn't realize that her almost unnoticed action did more to harm race relations than it actually protected her from a black man who she thought might harm her. In the plush downtown office buildings where I do my daily work, white women at times skip rides on elevators to avoid ascending alone with me.

I wish I could tell you that I believed that the parking attendant was proceeding in an innocent manner, or that it is a coincidence that some white women still react to me as if I am the "bogeyman," but I can't. I have endured similar encounters ever since I can remember. When I was eleven years old and visiting a beach resort in Delaware on a summer camp trip, the white shopkeepers immediately accused us all (black children) of shoplifting the moment we entered their stores. They made us leave their stores despite the fact that some of us had money and wanted to purchase something. At the time I was too young to understand how absurd that experience actually was.

Police officers over the years have pulled me over numerous times for no reason at all. Most of my black male friends can recall several incidents in which the police have pulled them over for nothing or followed them for several miles in the city. Of course, the surveillance black men receive from police officers is on top of all the other silly slights we confront daily from people who will tell you in a second that they are not prejudiced or racist.

I rarely repeat the racial slights I experience to anyone. What's the use? I do not want to be labeled paranoid. However, because these events continue to occur under the same circumstances and possess the same potentially explosive racial attributes, I have to believe that all of these events occurred because of racial attitudes. I'm reminded of a legal principle I learned in law school called *res ipsa loquitur,* which means "the thing speaks for itself." When a certain, highly unlikely event occurs, it can be inferred that it happened "more likely than not" because of negligence. It is a very logical principle. With regard to American society, it is "more likely than not" that racism (racial attitudes) leads to bad, occasionally tragic moments for black men.

I have to state it this way because racism these days is often unexplainable, although its manifestations are fairly obvious if you are black. I wish I could make the average white American understand what I am describing but it is difficult to put into words how entrenched racism (in its diluted, covert form) has become in the modern era. I am like that cop who uses a radar gun to clock a car going ninety-five miles per hour in a twenty-five-mile-per-hour zone, but walks up to the car knowing he didn't really need a radar gun to ascertain that the driver was speeding. It was apparent just by looking at the car zoom pass.

However, I want to stress that it doesn't really bother me that white women lock their car doors or refuse to enter elevators with me, or that parking lot attendants check me out with excessive zeal. I don't dwell on racially motivated insults too much anymore. Johnny Gonzalez, a narcotics detective on the New York City police force, put slights of this kind in their proper place when the New York Times asked him about racism. "You could go crazy trying to get to the bottom of every slight," Gonzalez said. I agree. However, I do worry about ruthless, bigoted police officers on the streets.

I'm even more concerned about the more salient evidence of racism's structural and institutional legacy. I reflect on it during all those lonely mornings I spend in Washington, D.C.'s Landlord-Tenant Court representing poor African-Americans and helping them to avoid eviction from their homes. Each morning I step into that court, the first thing I see is rows and rows of black people. Women and children. Men who have lost their jobs. Old black women on fixed income. The working poor and the very poor. I see the same faces much of the time, because racism and economic hardship often go hand in hand and never seem to lose their hold on some communities, people, and families.

Then I see the attorneys who represent the affluent landlords of the city. Nearly all of the lawyers are white males. To the best of my knowledge, many of them represent companies owned and operated by white people who own lots of property in the city. Usually they are upbeat; court cases for them mean more money. The lawsuits they file and the hundreds of black people they evict each year provide them with steady income. Some acquire planes and boats with their cash; others take ski trips or cruises. They are dressed impeccably too: designer suits, shiny shoes, beautiful ties, cuff links. This is the kind of scene along the color line that worries me more than silly slights. A scene that suggests to me that there is something terribly wrong with a society in which most of the individuals being sued for eviction are poor and black and almost all of the lawyers doing the suing are afflu- ent white men working for wealthy white-owned companies.

I know it has been said thousands of times by hundreds of differ- ent people, but it is our history: White people had a running start in America. Slavery, Jim Crow, racial covenants in housing, discrimina- tion, redlining, all of it and more got some white people off to a quick start while a lot of black people were locked inside the starting gate, confined and restricted, waiting for a chance to start running. By the time black people entered the race, a lot of us (not all but many) were way behind; the skills we possessed eroded or rendered useless and the prospect of obtaining the new skills necessary for survival in a capital- istic society virtually nonexistent. Thus, the scene in the housing court each morning.

Then there is the hallway of the courthouse, where I have sat hun- dreds of times. Although I do civil litigation, not criminal defense work, I always see the same thing: a parade of young black men walk- ing down the hall headed for criminal court. This goes on all morning. I sit there with my suit and tie on and many of these young men do not notice me at all. Yet I notice them. How do I know they are headed for court? Believe me, I know. I watch these young men shamefully ease into the courtrooms to answer charges, stand proud for their brief hearings, and then head back out into the world to savor an elusive freedom.

I know it is not much different in other American cities where there is a thriving crack cocaine market, mandatory minimum sentencing, and lots of young black men. But I am also certain that this is no accident. Using mandatory minimum-sentencing laws, America has effectively locked up thousands, perhaps millions, of black men for extended periods for nonviolent drug offenses. This tragedy has unfolded in an era that black people once thought would hold so much promise after the legislative gains of the civil rights movement.

Much of the blame for these alarming incarceration rates for black men has to be dropped at the feet of those who chose to become involved in America's flourishing illegal drug trade—the black men themselves. What you hear now in defense of black people locked up on drug charges is that the drugs were brought here by "da man." This rationale was best answered in court one day by a young black woman as I again waited among the mass of black men and women fighting for their legal lives. She was arguing with a black man about the drug trade in the black community, and he invoked this familiar argument. He was adamant too: Black people didn't bring drugs to America or to the black community, he insisted. They were incapable of importing drugs to America because they didn't own any planes, trucks, or boats. This argument has recently become the familiar final statement of some of D.C.'s veteran drug merchants right before their respective judges sent them to jail forever for violating America's RICO laws.

"They bring it here," the black man yelled that day in court, "they bring the poison to us, to our neighborhood." The young woman, who was in court awaiting the release of a relative, replied forthrightly. Nearly everyone in the courthouse hallway turned and heard her minilecture and took notice.

"They bring the poison here, but we don't have to take it," she said, "that's the problem. I don't care how bad things are, we still don't have to drink the poison. Nobody is making us drink it." I saw a few older folks in attendance nod their heads at the young lady as if to say "Amen" when she finished speaking. I would never take such a statement lightly, although I just do not believe it is that simple. Deep down, I believe that black American men are incarcerated at alarming rates because that is what the country wants. This has historical precedent too.

Immediately after the Civil War, in a period when black people felt particularly hopeful, America began to lock up thousands of black men and put them in prison on all kinds of charges. The plantation system was no longer existent and black men roamed the country in search of work. Having been turned out into the world with few or no marketable skills and unable to support their families, many of them stole to survive. In Louisiana, for example, right after the Civil War the prison population went from being almost completely white to being majority black in fewer than twenty years. After the civil rights movement, it seems that America has again decided to lock up as many black men as possible. Maybe not all of us, but enough of us to ensure that the policy is going forward mightily.

Critical to racism's durability is its talent for adapting to changing times, reemerging in new, insidious forms. Consider, for instance, the call by conservatives and others for a "color-blind" society in the spirit of Martin Luther King Jr. Somehow, America is supposed to snap its fingers, declare itself color-blind, and all of a sudden everything is racially equitable. J. Skelly Wright, an activist jurist on the federal courts for decades, dismissed the color-blind concept as a "meaningless abstraction." It is. But this is a concept that many (white) Americans now endorse and desire because being neutral holds advantages. Neutrality sounds fair only if you accept the contention that racism, as a structural, systemic problem that denies opportunity and equality to black people, has been effectively neutralized. I do not accept that premise.

Writer-activist Angela Davis has described racism in modern America as "less obvious but more treacherous." This is probably as good a description as I have heard. It also helps to explain why complaints from black people about being oppressed can be dismissed more easily. Racism isn't so obvious anymore because a lot of people have worked hard to correct their behavior, but institutional self-improvement is less forthcoming. People can stop saying "nigger" or stop believing that a certain race of people is subhuman; institutions find it more difficult. Colleges, universities, and schools can't change what they teach overnight and many, despite what they know, refuse to change. The media move slowly too. Television news producers have no time to deeply analyze the complex reasons why black men commit crimes or why black test scores on standardized examinations are low (maybe they don't want to anyway); they run their sound bites each night and let the public sort it out. I don't need to mention the fictional television programs and large-screen follies that come out of Hollywood. Some believe that the latter is most destructive when it comes to shaping racial attitudes and opinions in America.

And here we are, at the cross section where education, history, culture, the media, the entertainment industry, and everything else about America intersect. It is here where the struggles of the individual get lost and the perceived deficiencies of a group become part of every member of that group. I am Bruce Wazon Griffith at Fourteenth and U with the gun standing over Patrolman Arthur Snyder. I am a carjacker, a drug dealer, the bogeyman. If I don't shave for a few days and don't wear a tie, I rekindle a bad experience someone had on the streets or in some parking garage late at night—although it is broad daylight and we are in some office building downtown where we both are employed.

I understand too; even when I am wearing my suit and headed into those hallowed halls of justice as an officer of the court, I am sure some think I am there as a defendant. I have run into old friends and acquaintances in court and the first thing some have asked is: "What are you doing down here?" Their implication is obvious. I get lumped in with all black men on many occasions and I cannot do anything about it but pretend that it is not happening. I know that many of us are labeled dangerous and the rhetoric is growing even more intense—even from other black people. It has become increasingly difficult to find a place beyond the harsh glare of misapprehension that frequently threatens to distort—if not overwhelm—our true identities.

III

In Richard Wright's famous story "The Man Who Lived Underground," a black man named Fred Daniels is wrongly accused of murder by the police, arrested, taken into custody, and beaten until he signs a confession. Eventually, Daniels escapes from the police station and goes to live down in the city's sewer system, where he makes fun of the entire world in a variety of ways. The story is very real to me because I believe that black people, black men for the most part, have gone underground. We want to live, to endure. We will still seek out our goals but mostly we will survive the best way we can. The best way I can describe it is to call it a coping mechanism that has proved useful during this era in which racism seems to have settled into society in a veiled form. This is a technique favored not only by the impoverished urban black youths living "hard knock" lives but also by black men in general: those of us who have steady work and income, who take care of or contribute significantly to our families, who obey the law, and who have high hopes for racism's erosion and eventual demise. Our choice of the underground is both subtle and bold and manifests itself in hundreds, perhaps thousands, of small acts black men feel they must perform to protect themselves from the wicked effects of racism and racial injustice. These acts collectively represent our way of telling America that we are still very skeptical of the current society despite the collapse of Jim Crow and other obvious signs of racial progress.

Black men symbolically choosing the underground has nothing to do with our status or position in society either; it mostly has to do with our collective mistrust (uneasiness some have called it) of our own country because our lives are still frequently devalued. I am not implying that black men are unsuccessful or hopeless victims either; we are far from it. We are highly successful, and in many ways we dominate

American culture. We are entertainers and athletes and actors and lawyers and doctors and writers and we are taking Giant Steps. However, though we know we are capable of being many things if we work for them, one thing we know we cannot yet be in America is safe and secure from racism's violent tendencies and its structural and institutional legacy. That's why many of us have gone underground for protection. There is no historical precedent that tells us we should proceed any other way. In fact, history tells us that we are actually being smart.

At the end of "The Man Who Lived Underground," Fred Daniels comes up from the underground and tries to turn himself in to the police. He takes the police to the sewer where he lived even though they tell him he is free to go. As he again enters his former underground hideaway, Daniels is shot by the police and falls to his death in the sewer. His fate is the kind of ending to our stories that we are determined to change. And we are, of course, determined to change these endings on our own terms.

THE RACE INDUSTRY, BRUTALITY, AND THE LAW OF MOTHERS

DAVID DANTE TROUTT

The subject of race in America today can seem like a vast but marginally productive industry, echoing forgotten talk of a "military-industrial complex" but similarly enriching the careers of some while diminishing the life options of others. The race industry is unshakably hierarchical in all the sectors it operates—mainly, corporate media, entertainment, academia, government, and the law. At the top are "market-makers"—pundits, ad executives, self-appointed lightning rods, loquacious intellectual types, scriptwriters, judges, political candidates, editors, producers, apologists, instigators, oversimplifiers, anecdotal opportunists. (On the other hand, "*anti*market-makers"— such as the obscure organizer who defiantly makes a local difference, or that deeply generous mentor whose maverick reasonableness almost changed you—toil in the grass roots of experience and memory, ghettoized into only occasional relevance.) The legions of market-makers serve millions the racial products and services for cultural existence. But they do it badly, crippled by elite ownership that hoards inherited gains and disinterested managerial ranks more preoccupied with the size of coming pensions than their duties to us, the consumers.

Yet year in and year out, the race industry survives, always promising to get better. It doesn't, and its decline is reflected in our poor communication. Sound bites, commercial interruptions, and a mesmerizing array of antagonists-turned-experts prevent us from getting meaningful race talk on talk shows; fear, short attention spans, and disingenuous convention degrade the quality of popular writing about it. The deeper we may try to go, the more we are met with snappy commodifications of complex social dynamics, such as the "race card" label. The broader a diversity of races we acknowledge, the sooner we are reduced again to "model minority" paradigms dreamed up by headline writers. Like a mindless barrage of trademarks ("color-blind society") or long-lost civics tropes ("all men are created equal"), the race industry treats its own subject like barely understood signifiers of national citizenship.

Although most race industry output is talk or its equivalent, talk is not cheap. It is expensive to reproduce and costly to internalize. Even well-intentioned talk of race can lure us to violent ends, subdue our outrage, move us to electoral cruelties, and paralyze our empathy with apathy. This is because the race industry sells, more than anything else, more racism. And when even its talk proves too cheap for its stakeholders' expectations, the race industry, historically, can deploy a military complex of its own: the police. Whether or not race really is a poorly run industry, racism remains institutionalized, most acutely through police brutality, its most seminal form. By that I mean that relationships characterized by social exclusion and economic marginalization between blacks and others in society are wired into institutional life, where they are reproduced consciously and unconsciously. For many who doubt this, police brutality against blacks in particular is a contemporary specter that takes us back to our most violent past, when the subordination of black people began with the flesh and with the blessing of white male–controlled state authority. But before I address the focus of this essay—the entangled ways that brutality helps to condition identity in our culture—let's agree to concede that what I'm calling the industry of race is the medium by which the institutionalization of racism is discussed—or ignored—in popular discourse and conversation. That's a problem for which I have a few suggestions, the simplest being a call for well-told stories and a return to the Law of Mothers.

As a law professor, I teach about many things, some profoundly boring, others more relevant and titillating to people in their midtwenties, such as comparisons between society and industry. Whenever I inevitably teach about race—sometimes badly, sometimes well—I am struck by the utter lack of intellectual orthodoxy that students demonstrate. It is as if there is no framework of truths, no passionately held ideological tenets to work through toward conclusions, just an awkward analytical free fall into postmodern nothingness. Too often racism is past, while race is immediate, and never the two shall meet; ill treatment of a person of color in an employment situation—even a job in the legal sector—seems never to have happened before. It has no referents. Maybe a bad thing, maybe an excusable thing, but not a racial thing, and if a racial thing, then an aberrant thing for which a measure of personal responsibility is probably due. Like, shut up already, says the mind-set.

But not so acts of police brutality, particularly when there are even the slightest elements of race involved. That's when a certain clarity overcomes the students, many not much younger than I, as if they are sitting up for the unexamined Selma-like moment of their lives when their heritage and, for some, their very bodies are summoned to black-white seriousness.

The lines are drawn thicker. On one side are those who parrot a sort of popular formalism—let's not call it racism—about the police when incidents of excessive force are raised: that cops are mostly fair, that we should not dare to judge their state-sponsored actions until we have worked under their conditions, that probable cause to do such and such almost always exists. This is a formalist narrative that codes an even greater array of beliefs about fears of crime, control over freedoms, and the proper role of the state as an instrument of ordering social life. It pretends a rigid rule-bound consistency while denying its own desperation. Of course, this is a formalism to which most black and Latino students I've known cannot comfortably belong. They speak their words uncoded. They cannot avoid talking about experience in long, detailed narratives of emotion. Having been stopped, frisked, berated with racial epithets, mistaken for criminals, or simply unwelcome, they feel literally colored by perspective and therefore fight abstractions that obscure the experience of a body being threatened or pummeled by officers of the state.

With the possible exception of abortion rights, police brutality is the one issue that appears to transcend the current apathy toward political protest. Protest is no longer so necessary or cool or impassioned for young people coming of political age. Many parents now don't have to discourage their children from something they're not inclined to do anyway. But a few nights after the Amadou Diallo verdict came down, my wife and I tried to drive home to Brooklyn, only to be detoured by an impromptu march on city hall. We stopped, parked, and joined the marchers. A smug phalanx of police officers encircled the mayor's fortress, arms crossed, assembled in packs of hundreds. The marchers were young and loud, good-looking to each other, fiercely angry. Moved by the mostly black crowd, my wife chanted loudly, too: *No justice, no peace!* I was characteristically silent, brooding, angered to be in yet another march like this. But I kept hearing young women in front and behind us, taunting cops in their faces. "Look at you, punk-ass motherfucker, yeah you! Beating down black men 'cause you ain't got no dick!" The more I listened and watched, I realized these sisters were speaking not to all cops, but to black male cops. "Little-dick punk-ass motherfucker! Hiding behind your white boys!"

Before it could all register for me—the scene of arrogant power in the night, the spontaneous collection of anger, the bewildering vehemence against brothers in good jobs still hard to get—I got a tap on the shoulder from one of the women whose voices rang out behind me.

"Professor Troutt," she said, a little hoarse. "It's great to see you here!" It was one of my former students. It was great to see her there too.

———

Because at bottom a conversation about brutality and identity goes right to the body, self-description helps. I am a black man who happens to be mixed. My father, who died when I was a boy, was white; my mother, a colossus, was black. I grew up on the border of Sugar Hill Harlem and Washington Heights, an area that saw crack cocaine emerge in the early 1980s, police corruption scandals that ended in indictments and police suicides, and, in the early 1990s, mass rioting over allegations of brutality. My physical features faintly celebrate my blackness, wink knowingly at whiteness, and sometimes put me squarely into the racial ambiguity of a Puerto Rican, an Egyptian, or some Haitian elite. To many people, I am many things—things that, experience shows, have little to do with myself. But I internalize the complications of race and work it to the bone of identity where its construction reflects a typical myriad of the unavoidable and the voluntary. That is blackness as self-struggle. Not just because of it, I can be easily angered.

As of this writing, I have not encountered blatant discrimination from the police, been arrested, or beaten badly. This, I know, makes me an anomaly and, considering where I grew up, strangely lucky. I have had a police weapon pulled on me only once; I have never kissed concrete. Unlike most of the black and brown men I grew up with, I was not problematized. That is, my brown body and high-octane pursuit of everything I wanted was not greeted with instant worry, reined in before it could get going, or tracked harshly into numbing obedience, academic neglect, or mindless rage. Even without a father, I was allowed to be all the boy I could be and loved for it. So, when a New York City transit cop busted me for using my subway pass to go in the wrong direction at the wrong time of day, I had answers. Unfortunately, he, a great burly trunk of a man, had big arms and hands, which he used to throw me against a wall, lift me by my collar, and test my lies. Fortunately, my lies worked. Challenging the ticket in court (with my mother standing between me and the cop), I convinced the judge to accept my story that I was traveling to an after-school drum lesson (true), but had to go downtown first to help a girl bring her tuba to orchestra rehearsal at school (false). I was sixteen.

As is more often the case than not, the brutality of that situation is subtle, but it remains my single strongest memory in wanting to become a lawyer. Locating injustice is always difficult, and we are perversely thankful for the easy cases. A favorite criticism by whites I have known is that black folks are often looking for racism and find it everywhere. (This may even be true, and if it is, it's not wrong.) As I said earlier, the difficulty is in the application of personal details, recognizing them, not conflating or exaggerating them, and ultimately internalizing them into a framework of justice. (This can also be a source of rare empathy.) Most racial injustices are probably structural, which makes argument about them intractably conceptual and historical and other things that are more readily analyzed through shared orthodoxies, like understanding racism as institutionalized. Ours is a society good at institutionalizing racism. We commonly accept grotesque disparities in wealth, support and encourage segregated communities, employ exclusivity and xenophobia to sustain wealth and quality-of-life concerns, and we lie about it regularly under the banner of remaking the past as a right of color-blind democratic freedom. The past, however, is remarkably re-*produced* in colorized patterns that subvert basic notions of democratic freedom. Hence, race industry consumers that we are, we bog down over racism, discussing it poorly or not at all—unless it's real personal.

My run-in with the transit cop is at first personal. It is a story of a problematized black (or brown) youth as seen through the poorly trained eyes of a large white man empowered with—he thought— unbridled discretion to do to me what he wanted in the name of the state of which I am a part. Today, we spend increasing amounts of ink talking about what is "reasonable" for such a state agent to do under the circumstances. It was never reasonable to lay hands on me. This is my body. What he took was license and a bit of my dignity. He was enacting a drama of state power in which we both had specific, predetermined roles. Assuming I wouldn't challenge his authority later, and assuming that publicly roughing up a black kid in *that* subway station would yield no repercussions, he could have at me until he finished his business. For my part, I was supposed to get sullen, act scared yet defiant, maybe say something "smart" (he called me "clever"), maybe get my ass really kicked back at the far end of the platform, and, most important, quietly prepare myself by such formative encounters for a lifetime of suspicion, which, in the extreme, would be made easier by a rapidly growing record of minor arrests that could stamp my institutional identity as a "bad nigger." That is, we were supposed to act out instutionalized rules of state authority and minority marginalization and stick to them. The problem is, I am neither suspicious nor bad nor anybody's nigger.

My coming of political age in New York City was filled with frequent incidents of police brutality. Beyond the very personal—consoling friends who had been unfairly detained or jailed, bearing witness to acts of unprovoked violence by cops on street corners—there were too-numerous reports of excessive force. Some of the names of the dead arise in memory like family members—Michael Stewart, Eleanor Bumpurs—because of a kind of affinity you had for them, their rightslessness and familiarity, their bad luck and unavenged ends. The stories terrified my mother. Fear teaches powerfully, and what scares your parents scares you like nothing ever will. So, these names came into her stories of warning like sad representations of a self denied—mine, if I wasn't careful. The victims were so much like me in one way or another, and there would be no way to explain my death if it happened so stupidly.

This is what a colleague of mine calls the Law of Mothers. This is also one of the ways that racial identity is forged in America: across the pages and headlines of daily newspapers. I read them voraciously, as if I were looking for myself. I studied the details and the arguments. I tried to distinguish industry—the often biased rendering of events by reporters—from institutionalization—the apparently ineffective rules governing police conduct and the interminable hurdles to criminal prosecution of abuses. As a teenager, this becomes *very* active reading and a certain putting into action of learning. I am not suspicious, my mother assured me. I *must not* act suspiciously, she warned. I have a body inviolate, I knew, and it grew angrier about racial identity just as it was learning about itself.

These are lessons for young men of color, learned through the Law of Mothers' quizzes, questions, and warnings, and confirmed in news reports. That wisdom of survival follows you around the country, to Los Angeles where my uncle sat me down to tell me about choke holds, to Detroit where my cousins recited what to do when cops dispersed groups of black young men merely for "bunching up," to Louisville where a son of New York was taught the nuances of saying "Sir." These are lessons about the self with a literal brutality that transcends the vagueness of what it might mean to be followed around stores, or asked for more ID than other credit-card users, or not called on in class, or paid less for the same work as if you wouldn't notice. Internalized hurts all of them, but hotly debated when you try to discuss them with others. Unless you have spent time walking in and out of a city's establishments, say, with three little black boys and sense the chill they arouse around them, it is very difficult to talk about the recycled conditioning that makes them feel suspect and others suspicious. The discussions bog down, despite the personal feel. Except with police brutality: The emotive narrative won't so easily back down. But what is the lesson if you do the lessons right—if you don't act suspiciously, if you genuinely respect police officers—yet you are brutalized all the same by cops *who are not white*? Such was the case of Patrick Dorismond, a Haitian-born man who appeared one morning in the spring of 2000 on New York tabloids, dead from a gunshot wound to the chest. Dorismond had wanted to be a cop and worked instead as a security guard. One day after work, he changed out of his uniform, may have had a drink with a friend, and went to hail a taxi in the street. A plainclothes police officer working secretly with two others in a "buy-and-bust" operation approached Dorismond and his friend and asked about buying some crack cocaine from them. This infuriated Dorismond. Words were exchanged, then came blows. The two officers acting as "ghosts" stepped in. Someone may have yelled "gun," someone may have yelled "police" (there remains some dispute), but the cop with whom Dorismond struggled fired his weapon into Dorismond's heart, killing the young father within minutes. The cops were Latino. Dorismond and his friend were black. There were no drugs.

Much was written in the ensuing months about New York City's mayor who, in his rush to defend the police officers, quickly characterized Dorismond as a bad man with a criminal record (Mayor Giuliani broke convention, if not the law, by releasing to the press records of Dorismond's juvenile altercation with another thirteen-year-old). Now that a grand jury has failed to find wrongdoing on the cops' part, I respectfully invoke Patrick Dorismond for another purpose: to justify my lies to the transit cop and the judge who dismissed my summons way back when. Missed in these two stories despite their profound differences is the entitlement to anger many "suspects" experience. Patrick Dorismond knew he wasn't suspicious that evening after a workday spent protecting people and property from crime. Indeed, he was infuriated by the idea, possessed, he thought, by a civilian, that he and his friend would have anything to do with crack cocaine, let alone sell it. I believe he was entitled to that outrage, and that many other people would react similarly, yet the cop pursued him long enough for a needless altercation to get lethal. Just as I felt cheapened by the transit cop's singling me out for possible wrongdoing when I was merely doing something New York City students did all the time—riding public transportation to after-school classes—Dorismond reacted strongly to being identified as someone criminally connected with the single most destructive substance ever to reach a community of color. Dorismond didn't live to learn that it was cops who had cast him in such light. I was much more fortunate. I lied to prevent those heavy hands from hurting me. And I lied again to keep the judge focused on those same hands once they had. I succeeded in avoiding the debate that follows Dorismond's legacy: bad nigger or not?

Why, then, is official brutality such a diseased phenomenon as to affect generation after generation of men of color? And why, if society seems to come around to the horror every so many years, do its dialogues persist in foreign tongues?

Because it's really important as a measure of oneself. The black body is really important to the white body, the two representations of each other's Otherness so intriguing, terrifying, revealing in the confused American psyche that *all* races join the idiocy from that starting point. And all the myriad encounters they might have or wish to have together are so complicated by slavery, peonage, mob lynching, white supremacy, exclusion, control, and references unexplored through political, economic, and spatial segregation that it is all too overwhelming to discuss well. We want to throw it all in at once. We want to be able to begin from the same essential beginning and march into subtopics that prove the truth. But we can't. So we are left with our separate bodies in joint space. Then the bodies overwhelm. Then the bodies themselves are overwhelmed, and mere flesh—black/brown flesh walking around in containment of so much misunderstanding and difference—becomes the currency of control. Control the flesh. In racially violent cultures like the United States or South Africa, it's always been easy to strike out viciously over the fear of flesh. It clears all abstractions, ends the arguments, cuts to the bone of truth, and reestablishes a deeply cherished order with visceral clarity. So rooted in psyches and cranked out in cheap industrial reproductions, it will not go away over lunch.

If I'm right about intergenerational disease, that doesn't yet explain why the narratives are so different and so stubbornly disconnected. This I'm less sure about, because the contradictions seem so obvious. That formalistic narrative I referred to, the one that reminds the cop critic of the fairness and hardworkingness of the police, usually concludes with the defense of law. Even when it concedes problems with individual law enforcers (for a long time newspapers officially called these situations "aberrations"), it resurrects the sovereignty of the law as a whole—the rule of law as the overarching principle to keep in mind, the safest house for us all. And here we get generally well-meaning appeals to due process and reminders to assume innocence until guilt is proven. So far, I am firmly with this. I believe in this too.

But the formalist response becomes as inconsistent as the personal narratives it often critiques. Take for example the gang beating by Philadelphia policemen—white *and* black—of a black man on July 12, 2000. A news helicopter filmed some of the car chase in which we see the black man driving wildly in a police cruiser, its windows shot out, and he is alleged to have fired a gun at several cops. (Law of Mothers: If you run, flee by car, or hit a cop, Lord have mercy on your soul.) The action picks up with the car finally stopped and a crowd of officers at its doors. The man, Thomas Jones, is dragged out of the car. There's no weapon visible. He is easily surrounded by, to my own count, at least a dozen cops. Once out, they simply stomp and pound the shit out of him for many seconds, until eventually the frenzy ends. (Mine is a deliberately unsympathetic account, except to add that the driver reportedly had already been shot five times during the chase.)

This time the clearest formalist response came from the Philadelphia mayor and police brass. Briefly noting the extreme nature of the spectacle broadcast before the country, they went on to warn the public against jumping to conclusions or, my personal race industry favorite, "rushing to judgment." There was a lot that occurred before the stomping that we did not see on film, we're told. Mr. Jones was a dangerous man who had been violent in his past and had probably shot a cop that very day, we're told. An investigation into the reasonableness of the officers' conduct will occur after a full and thorough review of *all* the circumstances.

What makes an easy case like this one not an easy case anymore is the power of even rule-centered narratives to obfuscate rules. Reduced to its essence, the police commissioner's comments strongly imply that the officers involved here may have been provoked into that level of force by the—we'll call him—suspect. But there's no rule that justifies such force even if the officers felt provoked (and, no doubt, they did).

Here's where the Constitution and the Law of Mothers make perfect harmony: No matter how bad your little sister taunts you, you're *never* justified in pummeling her because you're bigger than she. Thus, if the driver were a serial cop killer who finally stopped to tell each and every officer on the street that he was going to kill their families with a chain saw, the police would be justified only in physically pulling him from that car, ensuring their own safety by disarming him completely, satisfying themselves that he was not resisting anymore, and arresting him. There's no special dis-a-cop dispensation for stompings. (That would be the Law of Gangs.) Suspects are not legally differentiated that way. Innocence before the assumption of guilt. The man had clearly stopped resisting once the car he drove was stopped. The formalist defense of the cops here simply ignores its own attention to rules.

By contrast, this is why the emotional narrative about police violence is more consistent than it may seem in its many details—and more attentive to rules than it gets credit for. Stripped to its essence, the emotional narrative says that situations involving men of color and the police are premised on rules of mutual suspiciousness, if not out-and-out contempt, born out of experiences. That assumption of suspiciousness is reinforced all too regularly in an imbalanced exchange, police power versus civilian whatever-you-got. Empathy for the stomping victim is not defense of his character or, if it exists, his criminality. But the police officers violated the law by beating a subdued suspect beyond the need to subdue him, and the police official's defense of the cops and continued attention to the suspect's past presents the larger issue with stark clarity: *They*, like Giuliani with Patrick Dorismond, assume it's all right to use state power that way. Whether these two narratives—formalist and emotive—persist in talking ineffectively at each other like foreign tongues is no help to the race industry unless we recognize the failure of empathy to discourage a climate for brutality. I say that my lies to the cop and judge were understandable *in context*. They affirmed my rightful dignity as a person in sole possession of his own body. I say that Dorismond's rage at meeting an undercover drug cop's profile of a crack dealer was quite reasonable *in context*. It affirmed—maybe too violently—his dignity as a man. So when I suggest that empathy could bind these disparate narratives, I am really arguing that *both* must own their racial consciousness in situations where it might be triggered. Only one does so directly, the emotive one. Race industry practice regularly permits the artificial de-racification of the (white) speaker, as if only "suspicious" people need make their racial status known. When more whites reflect first upon their own probable feelings if stuck in those experiences (core empathy), and next explore whether that reaction is altered when they inevitably reexamine the incident through a racial lens (racial empathy), then we might really get somewhere. We'd be imagining each other's different experiences more broadly and sharing humanity. The basic rules and principles, I've argued, are not the most serious problem dividing perspectives. The willingness to reflect against oneself a lot of historical and experiential *context* is. Hardly radical, this is the Law of Mothers.

Being a lawyer, law professor, or law student doesn't help you make these observations any better than anyone else who knows them personally (in fact, because empathy is unpopular with most laws, it sometimes hurts). In this country, police officers are only recently being charged with criminal acts in connection with excessive force, and the historically marginal successes now occurring in American courtrooms have little to do with the race of the lawyer bringing the prosecution or civil case (Johnnie Cochran notwithstanding). In fact, another primordial feature of police brutality is its relative immunity from the rule of law in a Mother's Sense. (Indeed, some might characterize it as the Law of Fathers.) This is a sad and complicated fact for many people who, like myself, first wanted to become lawyers to restore law to the injustices we experienced. Without defending her (there is no defense), you heard my former student turned lawyer. She couldn't even yell at the right cops.

What can be done about a primordial pattern of police abuses against men of color that survives with the power of industry and the sanction of institutional racism? I have provided various prescriptions in earlier writings, much of it legal and academic. The often-raised issue of officer training cannot be overstated. It has a sanitary tenor, though, as if its proponents were suggesting something technical, remedial, and not too serious. But better officer training for some cops actually reinforces the notion that a great many cops don't need it. Most of us come from working- and lower-middle-class communities in which a significant number of resolute, professional, and honorable young men and women went on to become cops. I come from such a neighborhood. I know and respect my former neighbors now, and calling for better training under the appropriate supervision indirectly supports the work and experience of effective cops, many of whom toil in work environments that make it hard to reach errant colleagues directly. However, training reaches only as far as prevention. As for remedies to existing patterns of abuse, I have argued for a much stronger federal role, specifically through the Department of Justice, for which there is ample precedent, important old and new federal law, and few of the structural entanglements that make prosecution by local districts attorney such a losing enterprise.

A third suggestion for eradicating the institutionalization of police brutality goes to the heart of Americans' increased identity as consumers. We consume everything—safety, agreeable perspectives on race, ice cream, property values, law school educations—some of it from private industry, much of it public. Like police protection. Within each city, county, and region, we consume the mostly public services of police protection, but often on terms that are grossly unfair to people of color. In this light, police brutality is one of the greatest rip-offs perpetuated against consumers of color, though we continue to pay for it. Here, then, is a call for communities to see such racial injustice as economic discrimination and to alter weak race industry conventions by organizing around that notion. We demand better service.

But the activist inside me always feels acute pangs of discomfort with such calls. They can feel rehearsed, a little redundant, tossed out without sufficient grit to them. It is the immediacy of the body at stake again. It is the knowledge that any writings about police brutality miss the latest horrors while they sit at the printer.

That urgency, however, forces a final conclusion that may further irritate an activist instinct. All of this is ultimately about how children are raised in a society divided by a poorly run race industry, and about how we each become students and consumers of its obsolete products and packaging. We have to raise more sensitive children. Since this is mainly about what men do, we have to raise more sensitive men. And they have to recognize the compulsion to repeat unhealthy ways of knowing others and to rein in impulses to act violently against their fears. This is as difficult as it gets in a society that promotes so little self-reflection, especially in the way one sees the Other. The "empathy card" has no real name and is often played too quietly against the institutionalization of racial subordination. But even the angriest white cops and their captains, with narratives turned inward, can learn it.

No life is cheap. Tell your stories.

THE BLACK BELT

How Justice Begins at Home

FRED MCKISSACK JR.

I am a child of the black middle class, despite my feeble attempts to deny it all away. I was not, nor have I ever been, a member of Jack and Jill or a black fraternal organization (although my grandfather dreamt that one of his five grandsons would someday join him as a member of the Elks). I didn't attend a historically black university, although my family has ties to Tennessee State, Fisk, Howard, and Hampton. I grew up in St. Louis, which, from what I've been told, has a less vocal black middle class than does, say, Chicago or, maybe, Madison, Wisconsin. I wouldn't know. I wasn't paying attention. I wanted to be the black Johnny Rotten, but he, of course, grew up really, really poor with hardly a glimmer of hope. My parents would often remind me of my fairly privileged life while I rode in the back of the Volvo talking shit about class warfare and the police state and the deaf-and-blind attitude of the Negro petty bourgeoisie.

So when I sat down to think about my life in said police state, I realized that my interactions within the criminal justice system have been limited to three speeding tickets and one odd day in December

1983 when the police showed up at my house. They said that a guy who sort of looked like me—between eighteen and forty, with curly black hair, light to medium-brown skin, and standing anywhere from five-foot-six to five-foot-ten—had told a cabdriver to drive him to the 5900 block of Pershing Avenue. The driver got conked on the head before the end of the fare, and was robbed. I was living with my parents at 5900 Pershing Avenue, having dropped out of college earlier in the semester in a bold effort to prove that I wasn't nearly as middle-class and predictable as they thought I was. Anyway, the police were understandably surprised to knock on the door and see me standing there, eighteen years old, light brown skin, medium build, and five-foot-eight. I was cordial. They were cordial. I asked what the cab bandit had been wearing, and they said a red three-piece suit with a white shirt and gold chain. I said that I would never be caught dead in such dreadful attire and they could check my closet. No warrant needed. Well, they said that wouldn't be necessary, and would I be so kind as to go downtown with them, sans handcuffs of course, and try to sort it out? Sure, I'm thinking. I have nothing to fear, because I'm not their guy.

Two hours later, my parents showed up. My father spoke to the detectives in hushed but I assume harsh tones, judging by the look on the cops' faces. I was sent quickly out of the station, sans apology, and into the waiting arms of my mother and father. They both asked, "What in the hell were you thinking?"

I didn't have an answer, other than naive phrases such as "What did I have to be scared of?" and "They seemed like such nice, trusting cops, kinda like the guys on *Hill Street Blues*."

My naïveté about what I thought was a thick line between guilt and innocence and the motives of the police has stayed with me for years. In the hour that I should have been Huey Newton, I became more like Huey Lewis. Had *Hawaii 5-0* and *Adam 12* so blinded me to police officers' actual behavior? Had it been the frequent visits to my elementary school, St. Roch's, by members of the mounted police? Nah. The horses were cool, but I was ambivalent toward their masters' messages. Several men in my family were in law enforcement, including my maternal grandfather, who ran the City Workhouse, and an uncle who was a postal inspector. Had their careers, and my adoration of them, diluted the customary—and, some would say, necessary—suspicion of police? Possibly, but unlikely.

After years of contemplation it has occurred to me that the credit, if you will, for both my naïveté that night and my minimal contact with the criminal justice system goes to my mother, Pat, my grandmothers, Bessie and Erma, and my great-grandmother Sarah. Because of them I've done nothing that could be seen as wholly illegal and unbelievably malicious in my life. (What I did to my two younger brothers was mere sibling horseplay, although to hear them tell it my good-natured bullying fell just short of Stalinist torture.) My childhood transgressions, after being told oh-so-many times not to do something, would result in my butt being tattooed by one of the staunch matriarchs mentioned above. Thanks to those stouthearted women, my notions of justice began at home. And since my whippings were delivered by the ones who loved me most, I guess I concluded early on that crime-and-punishment was a process steeped in fairness and a genuine desire to do the right thing. I had no reason to suspect that policemen were not as likely to say, before attending to their business, "This is going to hurt us more than it's going to hurt you."

My frequent journeys down the road of corporal punishment always began with an all-too-familiar scenario: me having a blatant disregard for the rules set down by my parents and elders. For example, after repeatedly being told not to take batting practice in the living room with a rolled-up sock and Wiffle-ball bat, I finally did what my mother always feared: I managed to shatter a very expensive, rather old vase. In retrospect, this may have been the most solidly struck ball I hit all season. Such incidents inevitably prompted a parental response familiar to any black child who spent time in church: "Tell the truth and shame the devil."

Oh, what do you say to that? I couldn't look my mother in the eyes, tell a big fat fib like, "No, Ma, I didn't break the zillion-year-old vase in the family room because I wasn't hitting batting practice with a rolled-

up sock. Must have been the wind . . . although the window is closed."
To lie, especially when told to shame the evil one, would be to solidify
the devil's stranglehold on my immortal soul. It would be like standing
over the body while holding a gun, gore splattered all over your shirt
and your name painstakingly written, in blood, on the ground by the
victim—and yet exclaiming, "No, officer, I had nothing to do with
this!"

So, like the God-loving/fearing/loathing child that I was, I'd bare
my soul with the sort of tear-flowing, slack-jawed histrionics reserved
only for criminal White House staffers and sex-craved televangelists.

"Oh, Mom, I'm so, so, sorry. I know I shouldn't have been in the
living room practicing my swing. I'm not only a terrible baseball player;
I'm an awful son. Please, please, please forgive me."

There was the smile, of course. The love of a child whose honor
hath shone no brighter than that moment.

For the guilty, at least in my family, no matter how repentant and
honest the child, the punishment was swift and solid.

"Thank you for being honest. Now, I'm going to get the BLACK
BELT!"

Three succinct, amazingly effective words: the BLACK BELT.

Okay, I've told the truth. I've shamed the devil. And now I'm going
to get the BLACK BELT.

The BLACK BELT was a size 40, with a standard silver buckle, that
hung on the inside of the door leading to the basement. My father
claims that it wasn't his belt. In fact, we didn't, and still don't, know
where the belt came from. One day, when I was fourteen and my
brothers were twelve, the BLACK BELT disappeared. Actually we
hadn't been whipped for a couple of years. We were well into the
phrase "You're grounded for . . . ," which was followed by a number of
days or weeks. In one case involving a deliberate testing of my parents'
curfew laws, the phrase "Grounded until your ass is ready for college"
was tersely blurted out, almost simultaneously, by both my parents. My
brothers were grounded a week just for snickering and listening in on
the conversation.

My dad never used the BLACK BELT. He whipped us only once. My brothers and I stole a candy bar from the grocery store. I was five, and John and Robert were three. We were in the back of the car when my parents asked us where we got the candy bar. We lied at first, then admitted what we had done. Dad marched us back into the store and made us apologize to the manager. Then he took us home and spanked each of us by hand. It really did hurt him more than it hurt us, because I remember the look in his eyes of both shame and horror. He told us that he wasn't going to raise thieves and liars, and he seemed to think that he had somehow failed as a parent.

My father's willingness to leave the corporal punishment to the women was based, I believe, on his respecting his physical strength. An ex-Marine and engineer turned children's-book writer, my dad always fretted about being too harsh. He worried that he would get lost in the moment, lose control. (That's the difference between being an alpha male and being a good father: the ability to understand your limitations.) However, this doesn't mean that my father refrained from administering *all* forms of punishment. My brothers and I joke that Dad was the supreme master of looking disappointed and ashamed. Scenario: We'd screw up (by, let's say, participating in an attempted coup of the seventh grade). My mom would say, "Wait 'til your father gets home." Dad would arrive, already informed of the misdeed. He would take a deep breath. Then, in a tone that combined Darth Vader and Fred MacMurray, he would tell us that we'd disappointed him severely, that his trust was misplaced, and that it would be a long time before the bond between father and sons would be healed. Then he would look hurt. And, for some really bizarre reason, we'd wish that he'd get the BLACK BELT.

My parents understood the difference between a whipping and a beating—and the lasting psychological effects the latter could cause. A whipping from Mom was tough, but ultimately we realized it was fair. We had received—and understood—the message that we could not set the agenda and "run over" our parents, that they were the ones in charge. The animosity we felt before, during, and immediately after being punished would subside within an hour or two, and we'd come to realize that they were right.

A beating is different. We were never beaten. I knew kids who were brutally beaten, and even though we were just children, my brothers and I were able to realize the distinction. For those unlucky kids, the animosity never subsided. This is not to say that they all grew up to be hardened criminals . . . only a few of them. Some have gone on to be cold to their parents and cold to the world. A few appear to be fine. But appearances can be deceiving.

Handling the BLACK BELT required the user to understand her own manual dexterity and strength, as well as possess a keen sense of aim. Bessie, my father's mother, handled the BLACK BELT as if it were an attachable appendage. She grew up in Alabama, but was moved, along with a sister, to Nashville, where she worked as a live-in servant for a family of devout Baptists. Among the list of whacked-out power trips that would make a child-welfare-services worker drool, she was forced to say her ABCs backward on a daily basis. She was whipped—no, beaten—when she couldn't do it. Later, she was beaten when she couldn't recite them fast enough. She never made me say my ABCs backward, but she remained a strict disciplinarian in a way only nuns and drill sergeants could fully appreciate.

Bessie, who died in 1995, and I had an unusual relationship. She was a loving woman who bore four strong, intelligent sons, one of whom would become my father. And as much as we both tried to deny it, we had many traits in common. We were both insomniacs. We were both headstrong and opinionated and had to have the last word. However, when you are in your early sixties, this kind of behavior is considered to be "in character." For a child, this kind of behavior is best described in the pejorative case. For me the SAT word *insolent* was used often. Bessie and I, based on my insolence, had several sessions with the BLACK BELT. These sessions were not long, but, to say the least, painful and memorable. The kids in my family were spanked in their bedroom, behind closed doors. When I was being spanked, my two younger brothers were not allowed to be in the house (this was the case for us all). For me, their absence was both bad and good. While they would be spared the sound of the BLACK BELT meeting my fleshy buttocks, and the yelps, they would also fully embrace the chance to tell every kid on the street of my plight.

"Ooh, Freddy's gittin' a whippin'!"

The kids knew what this meant. You see, the BLACK BELT had reached legendary status among the children of Pershing Avenue. Kids would come over and want to see the BLACK BELT.

"Hey, Mom Bess, can you show us the BLACK BELT?" they timidly asked.

"Yes, child."

She'd open up the basement door, and there it was. The long, size 40 belt from hell. It was so black that it sucked in all the light and air around it. The shiny, heavy silver buckle would crash against the wooden door, making the totally surreal scene even more chilling.

While the BLACK BELT was my elders' chosen method for taming my streaks of bad craziness, for my white friends from Catholic school, punishments ranged from the "good talking to" to variations of "sit in the corner/wash your mouth out with soap" (the latter was for crimes of speech or thought). To me their options were far too situational, and in some cases too easy. I had more than a few friends who would curse not only in front of their parents, but also *at* their parents. When a black kid witnesses, as I did, a white kid turn to a parent and say, "I don't feel like cleaning my damn room," and all the child gets is a mouthful of soap, he can't help but think, "How easy is that." Why? Because as recently as the last decade, for a black child to curse at his parent could be reasonably regarded as a suicidal act. Indeed, the daring youngster could wind up seeing a child psychologist and facing the following question, "Did you intend to end your life when you called your Mom a bitch?"

We were, I think, pretty lucky to get just the BLACK BELT. Other kids on my block swore that they got whipped with things as utilitarian as a wooden spoon to such exotic household items as extension cords, flimsy house shoes, and, in one case, a razor strop. I also knew, and sympathized, along with my parents, with kids who had to dodge phone directories, dictionaries, and other items not designed for throwing at anyone. My parents and elders believed in discipline, not torture. They were not eager to whip but they were thorough and just when they did. It was always fairly quick—a couple of lashes to the butt although my mother had no aim whatsoever. In fact, her strike zone was of baseball proportions, and once I think she actually hit an ankle.

For my mother's mother, Erma, and my mother's grandmother, Sarah, it was all about the switch. A whipping via the switch is a late spring–early summer thing. The limbs are in good shape then, and the limbs of fruit trees make the best switches. But the punishment is not the worst part about getting your butt tanned with a switch. No, it's going to get the switch that makes this particularly gruesome. You have to go out to the tree, peel or cut the limb, and walk it back. God forbid that you should come back with anything less than a truly stellar implement of switchmanship. Your failure to choose a satisfactory tool would require the whipper to get up (and in the South and Midwest, on a hot summer day, this is a huge task) and get another switch. This only raised the level of pain applied to your butt, thighs, and calves, because this also gave the said whipper time to think about all the other crap you'd done of late.

And then it would get good to them. They'd talk to you while they whipped you, asking rhetorically why you did what you did. At least I assumed it was rhetorical.

"How many times (hit) did I (hit) tell you (hit) not to (hit) [insert stupid act, followed by another lash to a fleshy area of my lower torso]?"

We would cry. And that was okay. I had friends who were told that they would get something to cry about if they wept, which I thought was pretty brutal. I mean, my God, what could be worse than what was happening at that moment? I later found out from friends and acquaintances just how much worse it could be.

I finally stopped getting whipped when I was about eleven. I'd like to say it was some act of defiance, such as when Richard Pryor famously told his father that he wasn't going to take it anymore. In his case, his father hit him so hard that his chest curved in on his father's fist and tried to keep it from hitting him again. My turning point was far less dramatic. One day, I just started getting grounded. Maybe it was because I was getting taller than my mother and grandmother. Maybe they thought an older child deserved confinement rather than a lick to his behind. I don't know. I didn't care. I've never asked.

It was the same for my brother Bobby. Johnny stopped getting the BLACK BELT when he was eleven, when he laughed during a whipping. For many friends whom I've talked to when writing this essay, the ending of the whipping was an all-important moment of moving from childhood to adolescence and young adulthood.

Was it worth it, whipping us for being bad? Should we have been given "time-out" instead? According to some academics the practice of corporal punishment is, well, not something our ancestors brought over from Africa. It is something we picked up during slavery.

"There is no record in African culture of the kind of body attack that whipping represents," Russell Adams, chairman of the Afro-American Studies at Howard University, told the *Washington Post* in 1998. "The maintenance of order by physical coercion is rare in Africa."

Okay, I'll accept that, and I wish I would have known that fact earlier in my life, because I could have used the information to appeal to my mother's Afrocentric sympathies. Despite Adams's findings, studies that I've read indicate that black folks, especially those in higher income brackets, support the notion that corporal punishment, when done right, is a good thing. (Okay, not just black folks. Late last year, a nationwide survey of one thousand parents found that 61 percent of the parents condone spanking as a regular form of punishment for young children.)[1] Could so many adults be wrong? Is there really a relationship between sparing the rod and spoiling the child? DeNeen L. Brown explored those questions in a 1998 *Washington Post* article titled "A Good Whuppin'?" She wrote:

> Many black parents see what is happening now—the dope, the guns, the gangs—and they wonder what went wrong. When they came up, it didn't matter what socioeconomic class, a whuppin' was a whuppin'—and it seemed that adults were in control. Now, old people are locked in their house even in the middle of the day, scared to go outside, scared of the young boys up the street. When did the old people, who would switch you all the way home if you did wrong, fold up their chairs and go inside? Maybe when the whuppin's stopped, the control stopped.

Such reasoning sounds acceptable in theory: A spanking, after repeated warnings, reinforces parents' control of their child while bolstering the child's understanding of the consequences of misbehavior—in the home and in the community. At least that's what spankings did for me and, I suspect, many of the kids I grew up with.

Writing in the *Chicago Tribune*, Salim Muwakkil offered a quite different view. Citing studies by scholars at the University of New Hampshire and Temple University, he argued that "corporal punishment is spectacularly ineffective in managing behavior."

The inability to reach a consensus on the issue speaks to its complexity. Complicating matters further is the fact that most commentators' opinions (including mine) tend to derive from their personal observations and experiences, most of which took place in a strikingly different time and place. Could it be that more and more inner-

---

[1] The nationwide survey was sponsored by Zero to Three, a nonprofit child-development organization, Civitas, another nonprofit group, and Brio Corp., a toymaker.

city black teens are running the streets because their parents are not much older than they and their grandparents are merely in their mid-forties? The scenes from my childhood described above—full of references to kind, wise, and stern grandparents and great-grandparents, a generations-deep network of experienced, revered elders—must sound like something out of an old movie to many of today's teens. Single-parent homes and latchkey children have increasingly become the norm, and it's hard to apply the same standards and expectations to families in such situations without sounding like some nostalgic, out-of-touch reactionary. You could whip heads from now until whenever, and it would mean nothing without a loving family, a stable community, solid schools, and the various intangibles that help instill a sense of hope and self-worth in children. I suspect that few of the teens who have traversed the labyrinthine corridors of the American penal system—the scary young boys in DeNeen Brown's essay—are equally intimate with such positive factors. I wonder if, for these kids, a beat-down by a parent or a policeman can be anything other than a painful reminder of their relative powerlessness.

Again, such propositions wander quite far from matters close to home, often expanding the yawning gulf between theory and practice. Will I pull off the belt or cut a switch when I have children of my own to raise? It's a good question, to which only time can provide an answer. I can only hope that when the situation arises I'll respond with the same discretion and good judgment that my parents exercised when they were raising me. It will be the only way to ensure that justice begins at home.

FEAR OF A BLUE UNIFORM

RM JOHNSON

I

Why am I fearful of the police? As a child I stole something from a toy store. I thought I was being very careful. I looked around the store to make sure that no one was watching me, then I lifted up my T-shirt, grabbed the chosen toy, and stuffed it in the front of my jeans, covering it. On very weak legs, I slowly walked toward the exit of the store. My heart was beating wildly, sweat starting to spill down from my forehead onto my face as I descended the two stairs of the store. I took three steps away, my heartbeat starting to slow, my nerves starting to unravel when I heard a voice.

"Hey you. Come back here!"

I didn't have to turn around to know that it was someone, possibly security, calling me from the store. And I didn't have to wonder if I'd be punished if I got caught, because I knew that I would. I took off running, as fast as I could, pumping my legs and arms with as much force as I could deliver to them. My heart was pounding again, loud enough to hear it in my ears, and so strong I thought it would tear through my chest. I was terrified, frightened, wishing that I had never stolen the toy, wishing that I hadn't been foolish enough to put myself in that position.

The man was still behind me, calling to me, forcing people that I ran past in the mall to stare at me and wonder what was going on. I pulled the toy out of my pants and whipped it across the large mall space I was running through, hoping it would catch his attention, act as a diversion, stop him from his pursuit. But he did not stop, and I realized now that what he wanted wasn't just the return of what was stolen. What he wanted was the person who stole it.

Just as I was hit with that realization, I felt a hard, heavy hand come crashing upon my shoulder. He yanked me backward. My feet, still scrambling forward, skipped out from under me, landing me on the floor. He dragged me back to the toy store, threw me in the inventory room where he kept me for two hours, interrogating me. He yelled at me, scaring me, this huge white man in the blue security-guard blazer. He made me cry, told me that I would go to jail forever for what I had done, and I believed him. I thought I would never see my mother, my sister, my brothers again, and I hated him for that. But I hated myself more, and I told myself, if I ever got out of there, if I ever regained my freedom, I would never make such a mistake again. I would steer clear of anything that could place me in any type of jeopardy with the police, because they are evil people, and once they have something against you, they can do whatever they want and be justified in doing it.

Finally, he let me go. I ran through the mall, stopping only long enough to see if the toy I had tossed happened to still be there, on the floor, in a corner or something. For all that I had endured, I felt I deserved that toy, and if it was still there, I would've picked it up and taken it. It was gone, so I ran home as fast as I could, trying to clear my mind of all that I had gone through, but I was unable to. I was nine years old, and the fear that man struck in me, the hate he caused to grow within me, I knew would remain forever. Twenty-three years later, the feeling has not left me. From that moment till this very day, I have never stopped hating the police. The catalyst was the power that man in the toy store had over me. The power, I felt, to do whatever he wanted, change my life—my future—and act as though it made no difference to him. I believed that if he had chosen to harm me, he would have faced no consequences for his actions. This type of impunity is shared by all police in spirit if not in fact, and is invoked at every opportunity.

This is why I hate the police, but more important, why I fear them, fear them even more than I hate them. The fact is that most black men, regardless of age, occupation, or economic class, have similar feelings.

If they themselves haven't been abused or mistreated, they know of a black man who has. As a result of such mistreatment, this excessive scrutiny and harassment, nearly one third of black men between the ages of eighteen and thirty remain under some form of custody of the criminal justice system.

Are that many black people unlawful citizens, or do they focus on us too much? Are we targeted as a people more than any other race?

If one were to ask Janneral Denson, she would probably say yes. She was six months pregnant when returning on a flight from Jamaica in 1997. After finding no drugs in her luggage, she was taken to the bathroom by customs officials. When she refused to show them her panty liner and the tissues she used after urinating, the officials became forceful. She was denied the right to call her family or attorney, and was taken to a hospital and handcuffed to a bed, where she was forcibly given laxatives and detained till she passed three clear stool samples. For the next two days she suffered severe diarrhea and extreme pain. Eight days later she was rushed to the hospital and given an emergency Caesarean. Her son was born weighing three pounds four ounces, and was placed in intensive care for a month.[1]

This event and events like these are why so many of us fear the police. But why are we targeted? Could it be because they fear us? Could it be that because on almost every television drama a black man

---

[1] "Woman Sues Over Customs Search, Claims Laxative Damaged Unborn Child," Associated Press Newswires, 19 Nov. 1998.

is always the assailant? Could it be that the majority of successful black motion pictures that Hollywood produces have violent themes that feature black men killing one another, black men killing white people, black men killing the police? Or could it be that every evening on the local news, it's always black faces that are being pushed into the back of police cars, black men's likenesses being shown in an attempt to identify the latest robber, rapist, or murderer? These crimes do occur in white communities, don't they? There are white people who break the law, aren't there? If so, why don't we see more of them? If white crimes were dramatized as much as black crimes, would white men be stereotyped as habitual criminals?

I see brown faces involved in criminal activity so often that I'm almost starting to believe that it's just us, almost starting to fear my own people as much as white people do. And what happens then? At a 1993 meeting of Operation PUSH, Jesse Jackson Sr. told his audience, "There is nothing more painful to me at this stage in my life than to walk down the street and hear footsteps and start thinking about robbery. Then (I) look around and see someone white and feel relieved."[2] When Jesse, of all people, has doubts about black men, when he is unsure whether he'll be mugged, beaten, or killed by us, why should we think that the police can be any more objective?

We shouldn't. What we should believe is that they are ten times more subjective. We have to assume that when police see a black face, they see the face on the news, the face they can't remember the exact features of, but can only recall that it was a black face. The same black face that raped that white woman, or killed that police officer seven or eight years ago. We have to assume that after they have pulled over our car, as they slowly walk up beside it, a slightly trembling hand hovering just over the butt of their weapon, they're thinking about the piece of footage on *Real TV* where a black man rolled out of his car, shoot-

---

[2] Mike Royko, "Politically Incorrect, But Right On Target," *Chicago Tribune,* 30 Nov. 1993.

ing with intent to kill at that unsuspecting officer. We have to assume that they believe their lives are on the line when they deal with us, and they'll act accordingly. We have to assume that or we run the risk of getting ourselves killed.

On June 4, 1999, it happened to a young Chicago woman, a computer analyst by the name of LaTanya Haggerty. She was simply sitting in the passenger seat of her friend's car when her friend was pulled over by police. Because he was driving on a suspended license, he fled. The four officers at the scene pulled their weapons and fired shots at the escaping car. They immediately gave chase, radioing in to their sergeant, omitting the fact that they had fired shots at the car. The sergeant radioed back, telling them that if the pursuit was just over a traffic violation, they should stop the chase. The officers ignored him, and when the chase ended, police surrounded the car and ordered Haggerty and her friend out of the car. The driver remained in the car, but LaTanya exited, while talking on her cell phone. The phone was mistaken for a gun, and a single, fatal shot struck LaTanya.

Officer Serena Daniels, a black woman, said she saw an object in Haggerty's hand and thought it was a gun. Officer Daniels and the three other officers involved in the incident were fired from the Chicago police force for reasons ranging from ignoring an order to end the chase to shooting Haggerty without justification.

Just one day after that shooting, on June 5, 1999, Robert Russ, a twenty-one-year-old Northwestern University football player, was driving his car. He saw police lights flashing behind him, but continued driving. Police gave chase. When Russ spun out of control, the officer chasing him jumped out of his car and smashed Russ's back window with his gun. Officer Watts, a black man, alleges Russ grabbed the gun through the back window, forcing it to go off, killing him.[3] Russ's mother, Vera Love, said, "He wasn't fleeing police but trying to

---

[3] Jennifer Vigil and James Janega, "Two Killed in Run-Ins With City Police," *Chicago Tribune*, 6 June 1999.

get to a place with witnesses. He was trying to get to a place where he felt safe and where there would be people watching." She went on to say, "He knew being alone and a black man being stopped by Chicago police, he knew he was at least subject to be beaten."

Robert Russ fled because he feared the police, as so many black men do because they've heard similar stories.

I have to ask myself, if LaTanya Haggerty hadn't been black, would police have yelled out, "Drop your weapon," as they do on TV police dramas, and given her a split second to reveal that she possessed nothing that could've caused them harm? I think so.

I believe those officers concentrated solely on that brown skin, and it sparked something taught to them or told to them by other officers. I can only assume what goes on behind the walls of police stations. But I imagine the dialogue being exchanged contains such sentiments as, "It doesn't matter if you're a black officer or a white officer. Color doesn't matter when you put on the uniform. You're not black or white, but blue. It's us against them. And never take a chance, never think twice when you pull your weapon."

But then again, I may be all wrong. This just might be the rantings of an overly imaginative author, a conspiracy theory that I've been conjuring up in my mind since I was nine years old, busted in that toy store. But even if that is the case, this is how I feel, and I wouldn't hesitate to argue that the majority of the black male population feels the same way. And if that's truly the case, then there's definitely a problem with the system. Even if every brotha' is wrong in his suspicions and doubts about the police, as I may be, but fears trusting them, what value are they to us?

II

On September 26, 1996, eighteen-year-old Jeremiah Mearday was walking to the store after having an allergic reaction to Chinese food.

He stopped to grab a few of his friends, and on the way to the store they were stopped by police.

"If you run, I'm going to shoot your ass," Mearday says he heard one of the officers say. Mearday dropped to his knees, threw his hands in the air, and told the officers they could put their guns away. He wasn't going to do anything. The officers holstered their guns, then pulled their heavy flashlights, and started to beat him over the head with them. Mearday fell to his side, wrapping himself in a ball, trying to defend against the beating. After the officers handcuffed Mearday, he says, they "came across my jaw with the flashlight," breaking his jaw and crushing many of his teeth.

The officers took him to a nearby fire station, where still hand-cuffed Mearday saw them washing his blood from their arms. He overheard them saying that they'd tell their sergeant that Mearday fell off of a double high curb while resisting arrest, and one of the officers fell on top of him. The reason the officers gave for stopping Mearday was that they believed one of his friends had an active arrest warrant.[4]

But what did that warrant have to do with Mearday, I asked myself after reading this in the newspaper. Was Mearday guilty by associa-tion? He has, in fact, served time on drug charges and has an extensive criminal history—but does that mean he deserved to have his jaw bro-ken? Was he beaten by police just because he was black, or just because he was present, or both?

And how about the case of Frederick Mason, a nurse's assistant and Navy veteran who was having a disagreement with his landlord? On July 19, 2000, police had come out to answer complaints by neigh-bors about this situation, and on the third call, they took Mason into custody and forced the landlord to file a complaint when he had no desire or intention to do so. Once at the station, Mason, who is homo-sexual, said that an unidentified officer pinned him against the wall in

---

[4] "Jeremiah Mearday Sues Officers Accused of Beating Him," Associated Press Newswires, 23 Sept. 1998.

an interrogation room. He claimed the officer handcuffed him, called him anti-gay names, pulled down his pants, and rammed a baton up his rectum. He said a second officer did not prevent the attack.[5]

This, of course, is just the allegation of a black man who was dragged in by police. But why would he lie? Why would he subject himself to that type of embarrassment if he didn't have to?

For the reasons stated, for the examples cited, this is why I fear the police. If a person can be catching a ride with a friend one moment, and be shot dead the next, or walking down the street with friends, then get beaten, have his jaw broken, or have a disagreement with his landlord one moment, and be sodomized with a nightstick the next, just because he had an encounter with the police, I believe there is definitely reason to be afraid.

When we hear news of this type of behavior from police, many of us are shocked and surprised. Maybe that's because we foolishly expect police to be objective in every situation, to treat fairly every person they come in contact with. We believe that they will be impartial, unbiased individuals who can assess an incident as no one else can, and help to resolve it in a fashion that is fair and just, in the best interests of all concerned.

If you happen to be a little old white lady, who has never been considered a likely suspect for a crime, has never been harassed because you look like someone else who could've committed a crime, well then, I can understand why you could see the police in such a manner. But I'm not foolish enough to buy into that myth, because I know that every officer on every force in this country, in this world, is just like me, a person. Nothing more, nothing less. A person who is subject to his biases, his prejudices, his fears, his beliefs (false and otherwise), his stresses, his bad days, money problems, marital problems, sexual dysfunctions, the works. It would make little sense to think otherwise, so

---

[5] Heather Vogell and Eric Ferkenhoff, "Man Suing City, Police Over Abuse Allegations," *Chicago Tribune*, 17 Aug. 2000.

I do not. Just like all of us have bad days, are short-tempered some times, so are police officers.

But the fatal difference is that they are given a shield of impunity. They are above the law, and in their minds I'm sure they are telling themselves that no one can touch them. But how should we expect them to think of themselves? They are given a gun and the authority to uphold the law, and to discipline anyone who breaks it, or is even suspected of breaking it.

Because officers are only ordinary people in uniform, I know they may sometimes find it difficult to separate their off-duty experiences from what they must do and think when they are in uniform.

Police officers are no different than anyone else, and oftentimes worse. That fact is evidenced by how many times corruption charges are brought against the police. Extortion, robbery, drug selling, brutality, links to prostitution. Not all, but many of them are criminals, so why should we expect behavior from them that is something other than criminal?

Is there a remedy to stop the racial injustices that are committed against black people by police forces that obviously think we are public enemy number one?

I'd like to offer a modest proposal: Let us police ourselves. We need an all-black police force that serves all-black communities, superseding authority of any nonblack force. Such an entity may be the only way to prevent our mistreatment because we'd be looking at ourselves, serving and protecting ourselves. Yes, I am aware that many of the injustices to which I've referred—including the deaths of Haggerty and Russ—have involved black officers. But if we were policing our own people, if we as black people were training our own people to be *our* officers, wouldn't we ensure they'd be more respectful, more knowledgeable of us? If there was an all-black force, black from the highest-ranking officer to the lowest beat cop, many of us would feel like white people feel when they see a white officer: at ease, as if the officer were a friend of ours, someone with whom we have something in common.

With things as they are, many of us distrust black officers. We suspect that they've traded sides, sold out, committed to advancing their careers by standing on the heads and shoulders of all the brothas they've incarcerated.

I often see officers cruising through black neighborhoods, their elbows hanging out their open windows, scoffing at black people, staring at them as if to let them know that they could cause them worlds of trouble if they chose to. That kind of intimidation would become a thing of the past. I imagine there would still be some corruption, but on a much, much smaller scale. And acts like the one committed against Frederick Mason would, in my opinion, disappear altogether.

If there were an all-black force, would Jeremiah Mearday have been called off the street just for being black? Would he have beaten for no reason after he followed orders and after going even further, dropping to his knees and throwing his hands in the air? Would his jaw have been broken? I don't think so. Because black officers wouldn't be trained to treat black people like that. There still would be black criminals dying at the hands of black officers, but I'm sure there would be far fewer unjust shootings.

Say, for example, that Officer Daniels was a part of an all-black police force, and when she approached LaTanya Haggerty and told her to get out, she thought about all the wrongful shootings that occurred when white officers shot unarmed black people. Say she thought about the nineteen bullets that ripped through Amadou Diallo, the beating that Rodney King endured. Say she thought about those things, because they were discussed during her training by her sensitive, experienced black instructors. Say Officer Daniels learned to see LaTanya Haggerty as being no different than she, as a fellow black woman instead of a mere civilian. And suppose she was taught not to see the streets and its black denizens through the eyes of white cops who suffer their own prejudices, but through the eyes of black officers who spent their entire careers policing their own community, making friends, doing business, protecting the people of that community. If that were the case, I wonder if Officer Daniels would have allowed her heart to slow just a little, her vision to focus just a little better, and would have seen that what the black woman before her held was just a harmless cell phone and not a gun. Would she have waited that one extra moment and not squeezed that trigger, sparing LaTanya's life? I believe so.

But the odds of establishing an all-black police force anywhere are too improbable to even calculate. It would mean relinquishing control over all black people when they have us right where they want us, as likely an occurrence as all the slave owners of long ago suddenly deciding to release all their slaves just for the good of it. I don't think that will ever happen, at least not in my lifetime. And it is a shame, because unless something is done, men like me will remain in constant fear of the men in blue. Even worse, because of the injustices that will continue to be committed against black people, there will be reason for this fear.

MY FLESH AND BLOOD

Black Marks and Stigmata

RICARDO CORTEZ CRUZ

"People should take a good look at life and see if it's good, you know. But if you got one person who's dead or dying or crippled or blind, then you have to say, 'It's bad . . . life is bad,' because you have to judge a tree by the fruit, and the fruit of life is a lot of people crippled, paralyzed, dead and dying, diseased. That's the fruit of life. So you should hate it."
—*Sun Ra in* Space Is the Place: The Lives and Times of Sun Ra, *a biography of the black avant-gardist*

Last Supper

Alas, one who is hungry does not care about death, and, sure as shooting, once you have tasted death, it's a lot easier to accept the whole thing. That's what I have learned, picked up as a rebel would rocks, in thirty-something years of *la vida loca,* of trying to survive in this crazy life, of being provoked by savage inequalities, of growing up barrio/ghetto in mentality before I realized that the time is indeed ripe to do right.

Now I feel like Richard Wright/Right—black boy turned into something bigger, product of the fears that a brother feels from America standing over him, draped in white, warning him not to write. Like Richard's, my stories are telling. With public praise and condemnation, I write up graphic accounts that focus on the alienated and impoverished black men who, without freedom and personal identity, make an effort to rise up. At the very least, I agree with Richard: Because of "the emotional state, the tensity, the fear, the hate, the impatience, the sense of exclusion, the ache for violent action, the emotional and cultural hunger," I "will not become an ardent, or even lukewarm, supporter of the *status quo*." Like I am right, I make it a habit to say, "If Edgar Allan Poe were alive today, he would not have to create horror; horror would create him." To racist, aweless America, *I am* "Richard," branded like cattle, as if He (I purposely engender America) owns me. Little things like browsing or buying at Christmastide summon my temper, tempt me to do wrong. (Black people can commit hate crimes, too.) "It doesn't take much," my wife, Carol, always says. Without her, I would be lost. Little things would get me.

The Death and Life of a Black Man

I am compelled to put my growing up, how my raising has affected/effected me, in apocalyptic narrative:

Friday the thirteenth is when the seeds of *not guilty* begin to unearth me, bring to light the things that have been done in the dark, the injustices I've witnessed or read about. I dig this idea of twelve black men sitting down at a table addressing/redressing life, law, and justice—sharing our beliefs, attitudes, and values, bound together through brotherly love, aware that what we say might be considered as gospel. I decide to do this, to speak in my mother's tongue, in the tongues of men and of angels, in remembrance of those revolutionary masses who have sacrificed their lives for social change. I see possibility for deliverance here, in this discourse, for the return of a dreamer. But this time "The Dream" quashes the American Dream. Our aspirations/ambitions will overstep the pipe dreams (the free-basing, etc., as a response to white people's X—ecstasy). We will transcend the paralyzing materialism, capitalism. We will go beyond greed, the urge to exercise power. Yes, power is exorcised.

Despite autumn leaves, this being the season for gala apples, and baseball talk of a "Subway Series," the fans are spinning, their metal/mettle working to cool me down. I strive to record my thoughts, lay down some tracks (ankles feel broken from hoops earlier in the day). Even when I hear ringing over and over again, I continue to concentrate, stay sharpened, because I see emphasizing righteousness and the importance of using good judgment as a point of exigency.

However, rings do cause me trepidation; I think of chains of oppression, echoes of the past, wash cycles where the Tide is turning and the time ticks off the moment for me to come *completely* clean concerning my emotional stains. (Herman Poole Blount, a.k.a. Sun Ra, but "Herman" stemming from his mother's fondness for twentieth-century Afrocentric magician Black Herman and "Poole" wildly rumored to be associated with Honorable Elijah Muhammad of the Nation of Islam, sometimes intimated that he hailed from Saturn, the ringed planet. If so, surely the ice must have made Sun Ra cold, made it impossible for him to completely warm up to people while on Earth.)

When Jabari Asim relates his vision for *Not Guilty: Twelve Black Men Speak Out on Law, Justice, and Life,* I am immediately moved by the view presented to me. I am genuinely impressed by his effort, but, more important, energy fills me after Jabari reminds me that I am not alone in my desire to find justice. Once more, I begin to believe in myself as a troubadour and trumpeter of God's will. My wounds start to heal at once. With faith restored, I am he who when he opens his eyes, it becomes light and when he closes his eyes, it becomes dark.

To my people: "I am proof that the oppressed can be raised and the oppressors can be judged. Drink from me, and you shall find elixir, strength in the understanding, the knowledge, that you can easily do what I'm doing—be a teacher, as well."

Biography

I was born August 10, 1964, constantly crying, ironically, during a long, hot summertime, after the passing of a civil rights bill banning discrimination, among the wave of riots. Heat-related deaths, including police brutality, drought, famine, the "summer of Sam," solstice . . . still, I was doing all right until I started to reflect upon the music CD *By George*—Gershwin's "summertime and livin's easy." With this tune in my head, I am near ready to collapse as I form the genesis of my thought for this book. I contemplate the robe/role of justice in my life, how struggle has skewed my vision, how all things have been created out of chaos. For Compton (south-central LA) and Harlem and other black meccas, the message always seems to boil down to issues of love and self-esteem. Or maybe the point is that my lashing out at iniquities is not ironic at all but rather a continuation of the sight/situation that I was born into. Maybe that's the goddamn point. I believe biblical exegesis will get to the heart of matter. I hope to suggest that the spiritual is always more important than the material; this is what I learned from my mother, and from observing my uncle Ted change his tire on the road and laugh about it, funning about the fact that it would be a long walk home and he could barely see with his glasses. Cuz Rodney and I sat inside the wagon, next to the piles of *Voice* (the newspaper that Uncle Ted edited) as he worked up a sweat, saying this was no way for a black man to go.

On America Online, my daily horoscope from iVillage astrologer Kelli Fox notes, "While a little pipe-dream can be good for the creative process, you also need to take care to keep one foot on the ground and accept everyday life." I never visited Uncle Ted at his wake or attended his funeral. Teds (Theodores) are wild in my family; there are at least five of them, all of them stand-up men grossly/monstrously steered by racism. I remember that my aunt Nancy had to ask for money to bury him. Rodney was like a brother to me, but I told him that I would not, could not, bury Uncle Ted.

Autobiography

How I got to be a professor, the rap or voluble conversation of academia, is a miracle to me. Though I have always envisioned myself as a young literary lion, lurking, ready to emerge as the ghost in the darkness, heavy stuff remains all over me like pitch, and everything gets under my skin, stirs me, to the point where I am too sensitive to even live, I think.

Seemingly always restless, I am nocturnal, blackest at night, as if trapped in the jungles of Africa, hearing the noise of a western sunrise, of a rattlesnake, while my world stays dark behind. Moon eclipsed by the Earth; that's what I am.

But, if detail can give insight into character, then know that strong-willed expressions of verve are my favorite things.

I listen to the jazzy vocals of Cassandra Wilson, dubbed "new moon daughter," as she wistfully sings "Until." And I, too, want the sweetness in life—"longing for the sweetness in life." Voice fades out, languishes, on this note. In a room of my own, inspiration surrounds me—theater-quality, coming from various speakers. I do not know how to harness the power. I walk like a Panther. Then I hear Somebody. He say, she say, "Keep hope alive." Hope is another planet, a different world, the bastard of our existence; don't you agree? When the Cosmos is swirling around my big head, and blackness is all around me and in me, and I am in it, Hope is the farthest thing from my mind.

In the meantime, I create *Five Days of Bleeding* and *Premature Autopsies: Tales of Darkest America*. They are novel ideas. Mordant, morbid. Stories that have me slashing characters and burying/forgetting them in plots like they were nothing. I become those ink spots, backed by nada/zero other than whiteness. This cat blacker than Miles, I search for paths to authenticate myself or to merely cross your path so that you will fear me. In my crib (that is, where I stay), the window is open. I can sense the mysterious violent gusts—untamed, whirling, scattering, moving endlessly—blasting through scrubs outside. All I see is curtains: black death, both happiness and prosperity plagued by violence. I know that I am alive, highly reverberant, charged with an explosive, at a time when the progress of emancipation is still uncertain, when the conditions that exist for African-Americans are not necessarily improved. Compared to many blacks, my sentence is light. I still have opportunity ahead of me; the summer breeze makes me feel fine. But, when autumn leaves come, I always feel *myself* fall, aware that I am no different than any Other. I survive, vicariously, through some sort of (or, some sorted) anger.

I don't expect the future to be brighter.

Coping with Life

Cipher this: Even the brightness of the sun can't change what bluesology black man Gil Scott-Heron and his Midnight Band called, in their 1974 lyrics of social protest, "Winter in America." In the generation of hip-hop, that song wouldn't be about the "*con*stitution," the destruction of the forests, and the ills of fighting, but instead about snow, cocaine, sugar. Just one motif remains the same: All people, everybody, know that the black man rarely has had a chance to grow. They know.

So the next statement is specifically for black Americans, to my people: Sometimes I get WASPs—I get the man—all up in my face, wanting to club me on the head with this same-old rhetoric that "life is better" and I should "appreciate it."

"What more do you want America to do?" they ask.

"Feel free," I think.

Contrary to popular belief, I was born and raised in the heart of Lincolnland, not Compton. I took giant steps to get to where I am today, to be liberated. But I'm still not free. And I beg your pardon, America (please pardon my analysis), there ain't no such thing as a release into the free world. Like a slew of black genius(es), I know my place to the point where I rage/rave talking about it. Here's a tip: Never tell a mad story unless you want people to think of you as, well, *mad.*

As soon as I talk to folks about my fiction, they ask me, "Why are you so angry?"

" 'Cause there are a lot of white-livered people giving me reason to be furious," I reply.

It's important to tell it like it is.

Rule of Thumb

You *should* change your religion, your way of life, or your attitude when a thirteen-year-old girl from your hometown dies on November 11, your sister's birthday, after being shot at a relative's house in the 1100 block of a street called "Prairie," in what police say was likely an accident or suicide. Because it is not good. I realize that these cases of massive brain trauma appear to be growing. But still, never say you're sorry unless you mean it; and do not allow yourself to get caught up in the idea of karma, lest you are wholly and altogether powerless. Shakespeare said, "Nothing is either good or evil but thinking makes it so." If I had read him earlier in my life, I might have spared myself a lot of agony, might have understood much sooner that even sinners can be redeemed. So today I speak with a touch of newfound urgency in my voice. Behold, I am a native of Decatur, Illinois, and Macon County (population 118,000, in about forty-two square miles), original home of the Chicago Bears. My whole life has changed because of that place.

Hypocrisy

I hate. I never want to think in black-and-white terms, that a person is entirely good or entirely bad, but I have always held that Decatur is a prison. Literally, several of the streets in my old neighborhood—places where Rodney and I hung out after leaving Monroe Park, where we schooled each other on how to play the game while our bright orange ball flagged cops and racist attention like wildfire—are now closed to drive-thru traffic. Bars of cement isolate/alienate what the city decreed as "drug-infested areas"; my guess is that the aged black community is responsible for planting flowers at the end of the road, where cars are blocked from driving in, for cosmetic reasons and to ultimately symbolize the morning/mourning of the dead. After all, you know what Malcolm X says about prisons: People will never reform; they will never forget the experience of the bars.

Located in central Illinois as "the heart of Illinois," thirty-six miles from Springfield (the state capital), and almost equidistant from Chicago and East St. Louis, Decatur—since September 17, 1999— has twice been the center of national attention. Of course, the most recent news is the Firestone debacle/slaughter, blackness separating itself and tearing up before eventually killing the people that had been cruising in control or speeding to relish their power. As usual, the powers that be claim they are innocent, promising to lay off many of the workers in its Decatur plant.

Decatur serves notice to us all that, in a police state and where the law is ineffective, wounds fester. Plus, where there is breach of contract, wickedness will exist. No spot/plot seems better than Decatur in showing repressive control over people. Because America wrote a bad check during its declaration of independence, poverty is perpetuating, especially in Decatur. At the mall or whatever, I see niggas walking around all of the time wearing a mask, like it is nothing.

Illustration and Color Maps

On the surface, Decatur is not divided like Chicago. A night stroll in this self-proclaimed "Pride of the Prairie" won't have you going down these mean streets. Then again, what do you say when your hometown engages in more saloon-type brawls—more knockdown, drag-'em-out fights—than the Duke, John Wayne? When it thrives on the type of climactic, gut-wrenching showdown, replete with itchy trigger fingers and ill thoughts of payback, that make *Gunfight at the OK Corral* a classic, a huge hit, for white people? When it features enough smoke and surrealism, hip gunslingers, to make even Clint Eastwood's spaghetti Westerns dull?

When people praise me for being nice (did they expect something different?), it's sometimes hard for even me to believe that where I come from is notorious for rustlings, robberies, shootings, and possibilities for fresh tombstones. My own mama warns me to be careful. "Watch your back," she tells me when I return to the house. She swears that the crime has reached a level similar to a "mini-Chicago," that expectant cops do not hesitate to get up into your face with powdered donuts.

"I am not steel," Decatur reminds me. Ain't no such thing as Superman.

What constantly rings true about Decatur is this: Though the town sports denizens meaner than John Wesley Hardin, its law enforcement remains shakier (I use this word to also suggest "shadier") than Don Knotts in *The Ghost and Mr. Chicken.*

I love my hometown (well, not really, but my parents reside there, and metonymy, association, is important to me); it's the site of poignant memories, the setting of my initial protest, where once, as a kid, I bicycled to a middle-class abandoned house, entered through a tiny window, took a quick look around, then stepped back outside in the bright sun only to discover Officer Charlie Irvine taking my wheels. "Freeze," he said. I was lucky that he gave me only a slap on the hand. If you ask me, same "pig" today might have shot me forty times or beat me down like Rodney King because tensions are mounting (with rising/thriving numbers of ethnic minorities intimidating our police force).

Statistics, the death toll, keep telling us that the number of crimes has decreased. Yet the vicious violence we've encountered lately, exacerbated by the media, feels epidemic, as rabid as hackers navigating the superhighway. American cities are rapidly turning into theme parks where most of us no longer have tolerance, patience, or hope for one another. People won't/don't give you a second chance anymore. "You slap a cop, you go to jail," luxuriant Zsa Zsa Gabor pointed out. And that's coming from a rich white lady! Imagine what happens to blacks who try slapping a cop.

The law in Decatur has lost respect. In this industrial spur sitting smack-dab in the state (I'd *like* to think of Decatur as the heart of Illinois), if you're black (pun intended), then you've already got a rope around your neck. Or at least it *seems* this way.

Authorities are constantly accusing at-risk youths of participating in "ganglike activity" and labeling them "thugs." The racially mixed mixed-up community of Decatur, once considered by locals the "Soybean Capital of the World" and "Home of the Jheri Curl" (think disgusting, drippy, oily, low-maintenance hairdo, and you've got the right one, baby), suffers while it waits for a savior. Because the city lacks proper leadership, residents' attitudes are (a)pathetic. Since the view depicts a lack of inspiration, no one in his or her right mind wants to go there and check it out.

The relatively recent event involving the "Decatur Seven" proved to be the last straw for me, the breaking point. The Decatur board of education approved the expulsion of seven high school students for fighting at an intracity football game held September 17, 1999. No blood was drawn, but officials claimed a seventeen-second tape of the ruckus showed felony mob action and a violation of its zero-tolerance policy, a policy the Rainbow/PUSH Coalition later labeled "arbitrary" and "capricious." The initial review of the incident proved to be opera, replete with orchestral overture and forthcoming interludes that only heightened the drama. For two weeks, Decatur became the stage for a national debate on zero tolerance in schools, beating us over the head like a drum major with these fancy/dancing ideas about discipline.

For the Decatur School Board (a board mixed with civilized blacks and not Negroes who prefer to be out in the field) and perhaps whites in general, there had to be stiff penalties for such criminal-like behavior. The sentence: life, a two-year expulsion for each perpetrator, later modified to one year, so that this gang of Monsters (see *Monster,* best-selling autobiography of a gang member, for all of the connotations and further meaning of this particular word choice) would never forget their repulsiveness. My sense is that, as far as The Powers That Be were concerned, hitting these black boys with the book, with the unforgettable pain of no justice, would ensure that these boys would walk around with no peace. In the board's mind, driver's education for these seven was now out of the question, merely something to laugh about.

From where I stand, Decatur's acidic/soured position on youth is just the midway point of so many things going downhill, turning bad. I mean, Jesus, you know you got "serious issues" (real problems) when Jesse James (I mean, Jackson) rides into your town with his posse/gang and leaves like Howling Wolf, crying like a little bitch, as "niggas" would say, crying like Zsa Zsa.

Watching and listening to Jesse speak afterward on TV about his recent experience with upsouth Decatur, tears rolling on camera, simply confirmed my suspicions: This God-awful supposed resting place, usually better known for taking as much delight in its blue-collar factories (Archer Daniels Midland, Staley, Caterpillar, Borg Warner) as Willy Wonka, is but a microcosm of a global/universal problem. That night I, too, wept.

To his credit, amidst the verbal and legal sparring, Jesse admirably vowed that he wouldn't stop pushing until the expulsion from school was rescinded for the teenagers. For an instant, there was reason to believe in the magic. Being such big stars and all, Jesse and his followers caravanned down Broadway (the street is now named Martin Luther King Boulevard) and stomped their way around thinking that in no time their visit would turn into a parade, a celebration. I have no doubt that they came with pixie dust in/on hand. Actually, I missed the show, but this is how I imagine the event and what I heard about it, how I now recollect it to those that ask me about it. ("The mind is a powerful thing," my wife reminds me. She is a joyful song, like my mother, strong and replete with harmony, and so I love listening to her. When she's not around, I find myself chanting her name as if I am certain that her spirit is everywhere, in me and all around me, even under the rocks that I pick up.)

They *stoned* Jesus, I keep thinking. I keep thinking about how it doesn't pay to be a martyr, literally or in any other desirable way. O, the mighty reverend and his cast of devoted supporters boldly stirred up a lot of mess in the eyes of the Decatur community. But the black cauldron was already there, back in the day when I was running the streets, calling the shots, breaking in and entering this white man's house. You can believe that. I hate to say it, but as soon as Jesse split town, white supremacist Matt Hale and the KKK put on a demonstration to protest the reverend's involvement. Even from Genesis or in every case of geneses, hasn't it always been like this, one thing begetting another?

In the end, I guess I am a Decatur product—homegrown, volatile, guilty of snapping and losing my temper in a heartbeat, exactly what most white people expect of a black man. I do carry a chip on my shoulder (no, not an Intel processor, regrettably). White people who have been victimized by my wrath might say that there's an even darker side to me, something less intelligent that makes me more reactionary than proactive. Frankly, I am just plain tired of being embarrassed by/of my roots. As they say in *Newsweek,* it's someone else's turn.

Demons

When I was growing up, in the 'hood, I didn't think about winter in America. It was always summertime, summertime for me. Outside(r), I waited for ice-cream trucks (ours was called "Mister Softee"), not people transporting snow. I held that there were delivery trucks backing up to the door of industry, not Black Marias (closed trucks for conveying prisoners to and from jail). Music producer and artist Puff Daddy says, "It's all about the Benjamins now." But Oprah puts it more accurately: "Racism slowly wears you down." Nothing has ever frightened me more than racism. Although back in the day, blue or blackish racers, snakes, usta to scare the hell out of me in the backyard, and *I was afraid* of the dark; maybe that was the omen.

Fortunately for me, by the grace of God, I never believed that taking the bread of life meant eating from one another's flesh, devouring my own kind. I never got into that.

The Apocalypse

We come to this. . . . Darkness seemingly covering the land, people blacker than a hundred midnights, black 360 degrees, our world so full of mess that we vomit on bent knee (black vomit), our world so full of chaos to the point where we feel jailed by it. I demand simple justice for simpler times.

With tablets/commandments for learning in the palm of our hands, teachers are like prophets, just wanting to do God's will, because He's allowed us to go to the mountaintop, to ensure that we as a people get to the Promised Land. Leopold Senghor asserts that "all change, all production and generation are effected through the word." I mean, in the beginning there was only the word, then God stepped out on space and said, "I'll make me a world." However, very quickly, He became bored with it. So God sat down—on the side of a hill where He could think; by a deep, wide river He sat down; with His head in His hands, He sat down, this awesome, gigantic God, staring at the Earth, at Disneyland, the mass of people, the ball that the Cat had previously hurled around and played with for amusement. Like a mammy bending over her baby, God now looked at it, the Earth (a small, small world at his feet). The Almighty knelt down in the dust, toiling over a lump of water-soaked soil, of soft wet earth, as if He held Play-Doh, until He thought of a new idea, thought of words carrying meaning, substance, form, the content of their character through which man could be judged. And it was good, all good. So into the word, God blew the breath of life. And God said: That's good, that's good.

Predestination

I cannot forget my teachers or that I'm obligated to teach myself. According to an African proverb, "[S]he who learns, teaches." I remember this one teacher, a community-college instructor, who accused me of plagiarism. She got all up in my face and charged me with speaking not in my mother tongue or my mama's tongue, but rather in the language and voice of someone or something else. "Your problem is that you talk in black and white, talk like a primitive television set, talk out the side of your mouth like a talking head," she suggested. Imagine that: me, a teacher of writing in the making, in huge hands of the God, plagiarizing or being accused of it, my big lips indicting me. The crime was initially funny to me. Still, this was an instructor that was not good for the world. Soon afterward, I found motivation, what every black writer needs, demands; it was that bitter, bloody moment of a Negroid once again being regarded as inarticulate, a man-child. Made me feel like an alien. "This prejudice hurts," I said to myself when I got hip. "Hurts." Like she had stabbed me with a pen, put a hole in my soul, you dig?

"Word, you've never seen anybody work it like me before, have you? I can read you like a book": I recall telling that to this pale instructor, not in King's English, but with an even funkier attitude, in black talk, spooking her, damn near speaking from the bottom of the well. And all the while feeling hurt 'cause she never believed that she could talk and I could talk back. I remember talking back, talking black. That was the day when I was destined to become a teacher, a soothsayer, fated to be my brother's and my sister's keeper.

Justice

Akin to love and grace; judgment of our oppressors so central to hue-man life that we feel empty without it; suggesting a sincere regard for the poor and the weak; necessary for one to develop a sense of community and for the preservation of that community; carried out solely on the basis of need; something that is promising; vindication from slavery and deliverance from evil; flowing in and out of those who believe; raising the dead. Justice does not always prevail, I am sorry to say (just ask starlet Halle Berry, Miss Dorothy Dandridge herself).

At the Cross, at the Crossroads

(Where I first saw the light and the burdens of my heart rolled away, rolled away) In the beginning, there was the word, the promise of "justice."

But now you've got a brother like me. Instead of sitting at home and watching TV with two tuners or playing Mortal Combat, we dwell in unfathomable/unimaginable poverty, constantly moving in and out of transit/transition, unsupervised, disaffected, unalarmed by who and what we are. We are black men in public space, hoping for a parallel world, but around and around we go, and where we stop . . . nobody knows.

For the lot of us who have witnessed social injustice and dare to fight against it, death is only a phase in the conflict and struggle, not an end. As I hear Jimi Hendrix's "Star-Spangled Banner" twanging in my head, the pluck of an instrument, I wait for the chance to truly feel alive, untroubled, without fear. I envision our King crowned and see twelve men in evolution, transcending ourselves to raise the dead. Sun, no doubt, smiling, with a rainbow coalition, a band of unity, these funky rays of cosmic multiculturalism (see the cultural work of music pioneer George Clinton for an idea of parliamentary funk) signifying the dawning of a new day. And I smell fresh herb. When we sit down at the table, we no longer have the black dog over us; we no longer fear the police. Everybody is together, in brotherhood, taking in soul food, thinking *Others first*. The bread gets shared while we drink from the cup of blessing.

As for your part, America, *hope and pray* that we have indeed become disciples of a movement to destroy the ruling powers of evil without violent upheaval because only then will we not betray you.

FROM WITHIN,
FROM WITHOUT

ANDRE JACKSON

I was twelve years old when the police first stopped me along a street of neat lawns and lily whiteness on St. Louis's South Side. My best friend, his older brother, and I were out of school on a bright summer's day in 1974, exploring the other, forbidden side of town. The South Side was a land of neat bungalows, colorful flower beds, and carefully edged lawns jealously protected by the "Scrubby Dutch" occupants who lived there. A lot different from the mostly black North Side, a world and a long bus ride away at the other end of Kingshighway Memorial Boulevard.

We were out on the town, killing a summer's day that, like most others, seemed to drag on interminably when you didn't have much to do. I was wide-eyed and full of myself like any other preteen.

My coming-of-age as a black man in America began when a little white girl half my age shouted something at us from behind a fence. I didn't really hear what she said, and kept walking along, "joning" and laughing with my partners. A moment later, my boy Charles told me, "You know, she just called us niggers." In those days, that insult fell often from white folks' lips, especially on the South Side, and usually when the vocalizer was behind the wheel of a motor vehicle and thus able to quickly escape without penalty.

Fully immersed in the belief of immortality that often inoculates the young against reality, I responded by doing the typical, cool, smart-ass thing: I gave the little white girl the finger. You know, the middle-finger salute. I'd like to say now that I was a righteously angry young brother railing against the racist system symbolized by a ruddy-faced blond white child. I wasn't. I was merely trying to have the last word. It turns out the last word was had by the two police detectives who happened to be driving by at that moment. Before my finger-giving hand had fallen back to my tank-topped side, their old, unmarked Dodge had made a tire-squealing U-turn and jerked to a halt beside us.

The two middle-aged men in their sunglasses, narrow-brimmed straw hats, and cheap sport coats concealing their holstered .38s jumped out and flashed their badges. In no uncertain terms, they asked what the hell was going on and, more important, what we were doing on Fyler Avenue in St. Louis, since the nearest black person lived at least five miles away in those days, way over on the other side of what impolite society called "Dago Hill."

"I saw you giving the finger to that girl," charged the taller one as I shifted from one implausible lie to another to cover my real behavior. "What're you backing up for?" he taunted. "Now, tell the truth before we beat your goddamned heads in," suggested Officer Friendly. "You know we'll whip on you, don't you?"

After a few minutes of berating us and writing down our names and addresses on official-looking forms, the two cops admitted that "we don't want to see you kids get hurt around here" and wondered aloud what would happen if they walked down a street in my neighborhood and gave some random resident a middle-finger salute. "I might get my ass whipped, right?" said one. He didn't buy my protestation that the North Side was a bastion of peace and love.

The two coppers again ordered us to behave and then drove away, leaving us a bit wobbly legged, shaken, and chastened on that neat sidewalk in south St. Louis. I was never quite the same after that. Did that chance encounter with a couple of rough-mouthed detectives send me off the pristine path and onto a wayward road of crime and degradation? No. But I never again looked at cops quite the same way. I never dated white girls either. From that moment on, I was wary of the police. It would be nearly fifteen years before the LA rap group N.W.A. recorded the 'hood anthem "F*** tha Police," but I might have agreed with their sentiment on that bright summer day in 1974—silently, to be sure, at least until the cops were out of earshot.

Coming-of-Age

I'll never know if that routine sidewalk stop resulted in the filing of any official police paperwork containing my name, address, and social security number. But it sure seemed as if the cops had it in for me from that point on. More likely than this personal conspiracy theory is the fact that I was growing up fast, heading into that age and physical size that makes you, simultaneously, a big black man and a threat to much of white America.

Not that I often encountered white America in my old north St. Louis neighborhood, known as the "schoolteachers' ward" for the large number of working- and middle-class black professionals and well-paid blue-collar workers who lived there. The last white family carted their belongings onto a moving van and drove away well before my age reached double digits. I never knew any white people my age until I went away to college.

To be sure, my zip code wasn't idyllic suburbia; the 'hood was only a short walk away. You could find it in the four-flats and tenements that ringed the blocks of mostly neat, three-story brick houses where I grew up. The flats and boardinghouses housed the thugs and bullies who tortured me throughout childhood, until I figured out that delivering a good ass-whipping—or your best effort toward that goal—was a lot less painful than takin' one. Although the police to date—knock on wood—have yet to lay a hand on me, I spent much of my early life fending off black folk who'd taken a dislike to me for no good reason.

I learned over time that cops will hassle you for being black; growing up, my own people hassled me for being, depending on the day, a punk, jive, or merely appearing to be smart. Intelligence wasn't cool in the schoolteachers' ward; still isn't, really.

Saviors or Overseers

This dual oppression, from within the 'hood and from without, has led me to a type of survivalist mentality that I've often glimpsed in black people who grew up in a manner similar to me. White folks rarely give you a break and black folks often won't either. The police might well be quick to cap me if I make a sudden move or innocently blunder into a tragic set of circumstances, but brotherman on the corner is at least as likely to mean me no good. Still, when somebody's kicking in your door, who're you gonna call—911 (yeah, I know, Public Enemy says "it's a joke in your town") and the folks in blue, or the boyz from da 'hood? I know which way I'd go.

Having grown up in a family of police officers makes my choice easier. Those who've sworn an oath to uphold the law have been numbered among my relatives since the end of World War II. The patriarch of this sepia-colored version of the Thin Blue Line was my stepfather, a man who, in his day of walking a beat in rough neighborhoods, somehow gained a sobriquet first granted to one of Teddy Roosevelt's famed Rough Riders. "Ass Kicking Dakota" was how he was known in the bars, brothels, and gambling dens of St. Louis's old Mill Creek Valley, a neighborhood that was long ago bulldozed and urban-renewaled out of existence. Long after he had retired from the police force, I encountered those who'd had apparently memorable misadventures with him. Once, driving down Martin Luther King Drive with him, I watched a group of wine-drinking old men quickly vacate the street corner in front of a liquor store when they saw his stern countenance. The old heads dropped their bottles and scurried around the corner as fast as their aged, arthritic limbs would move them. "You see that Negro?" Dakota said, taking his hand off the wheel of his big, policelike sedan to point toward one of the men. "I locked him up in 1947."

Dakota wasn't any easier on whites, to hear him tell it. He and his partner once emptied their guns into a car full of white men after they dissed him and a fellow black cop and tried to run them down. As best as they could tell, no one was hit by their gunfire, but they never again saw that group of drunken whites in the black part of town.

Besides Dakota, other cop relatives were part of my childhood experiences. My grandmother regularly clipped newspaper articles chronicling the daring exploits of my uncle, the detective, who seemed to collar some infamous murderer every week. Another relative, a sheriff's deputy, regularly made the news after he became warden of the city jail for a time in the '70s. Two cousins my age have joined the police force.

Having role models in your family who represented the good side of the police made it hard to hate all cops. If N.W.A. had been singing in the '70s, I would have been real confused.

I wouldn't be confused, though, then or now, about police brutality. I have no tolerance for police killings that have no plausible explanation, such as the death of Amadou Diallo. Nearly four times as many bullets struck him (not counting those slugs that missed) as Utah loads into the weapons of its prison firing squad. Missouri law governing the death penalty requires that the crime be "outrageously wanton and vile." To me, as an outside observer, the Diallo case and others like it fit that description. Such outrageous cases of police overreaction make it easy, too easy, to mistrust all cops. To me, that's just like white America's continual judging of black people not by our successes, but by the lowest among us. The truth, as in much of life, is at neither extreme, but somewhere in between. Through the years, I've run across more decent cops than bad ones.

Growing into a Profile

My relatives' brethren in blue aren't all good, though. I knew that from my first encounter with the law boys. Unfortunately, that lesson kept repeating itself, even though I learned it full well the first time.

At twelve years of age, I stood six feet tall and, peach fuzz on my chin notwithstanding, I looked a lot older than I was. To many who refused to see beyond their racist perceptions, I became a big, powerful threat, even though I was really just a lanky, goofy teenager. Being black didn't help, in the eyes of the lawmen, and lawwomen.

My encounters with cops increased in frequency as I grew older. As a young teen, being black and in the general vicinity was enough to make a musty-smelling shopping mall rent-a-cop associate me with a gang of young brothers he'd detained for some offense, even though I'd never seen any of them before. Hell, twenty miles and a river likely separated our neighborhoods. Luckily, the chief suspect denied knowing me when the security guard asked, "Was he with you?" I might have avoided a trip to juvenile hall that day.

Growing into young adulthood made me even more of a target for police stops. I've lost count of how many times I've been stopped. I quickly learned the survival rules for a young black man that take effect when the flashing lights and spotlights are trained your way: stop, move your hands slowly into plain view, speak slowly and clearly, acknowledge any instructions from police, keep your temper in check, and do what you're told. As a Supreme Court Justice once memorably remarked, midnight on the side of a road is not the time to debate your civil rights with a cop. That can come later, after you've survived the encounter.

Other Lessons

You grow up quick in the 'hood. You grow hard quick, too. I often think back to the wasted lives and wasted potential of too many people I've known. You've heard it before from other voices, but it's no exaggeration to say that a frighteningly high percentage of people I grew up around are imprisoned, dead, or dying. In the words of author Jill Nelson, I've had too many "authentic Negro experiences."

Take my usually violent adventures with a neighborhood thug named Rob, who often ran with his pimply-faced half brother with the different last name. At the age when many kids are worrying about how they'll face their future in high school, I spent much of the seventh and eighth grades alternately avoiding this pair, or tussling with them. At stake were, at varying times, the few coins that comprised my lunch money, my bicycle, my ass, and, not least of all, my pride. Rob and his brother were no strangers to juvenile hall; they were infamous in the neighborhood for allegedly burglarizing a tire store. Since they weren't old enough to drive, I still marvel over what they were looking to steal. After scattered episodes of cursing and flying fists, which usually resulted in me being the loser, they followed their mama and moved away.

The next time I ran across Rob was when I saw his mug shot in the newspaper, underneath a headline announcing the arrest of a teen described as a "one-man crime wave." He was facing a long stay in what I once heard a black judge describe as the "Great Sodomy House in Jefferson City." I'd like to say I felt sorry for the "brother," but why lie?

Little had changed by the time I entered high school in 1975. I spent a good portion of freshman year fighting at Charles Sumner High School. Brawling was sort of an unofficial B-team and varsity sport at Sumner, lending an ironic, tragic dissing to a school steeped in African-American history.

Sumner, graduates proudly note, was the first free secondary school for African-Americans between the Mississippi River and the

Pacific Ocean. Since its founding a decade after the soldiers of the Civil War had laid down their weapons, Sumner has remained a focal point of the black community in St. Louis. Pop singer Tina Turner and opera diva Grace Bumbry, the late tennis great Arthur Ashe and activist Dick Gregory are all counted among its alumni.

Much of that glory had left along with the middle class by the time I got there. Sumner High, in 1975, counted more than a half-dozen guards on its payroll. Long before the high school massacre at Littleton, Colorado, entered the nation's consciousness, my old school housed a police substation down the hall from the principal's office.

Besides the usual adolescent fear of the clanging lockers and crowded hallways that mark entry to high school, I had more serious matters to worry about. The year I was finishing eighth grade was the year a Sumner student had been shot to death at school after refusing to give up his leather coat to a robber. A neighbor girl who had entered Sumner the year before suffered serious stab wounds as the result of an all-girl brawl. A rough-customer cousin who had preceded me to Sumner found herself staring at a butcher knife as the result of another altercation at the school.

While I worried about my safety at Sumner, my neighborhood wasn't faring much better. The summer before I started high school was marked by the brutal murder of the big sister of a friend of mine. The girl, whom I had a secret crush on, was stabbed repeatedly by a spurned boyfriend. I doubt she was even seventeen when she died in her home.

With events like these going on around me, the police became the least of my worries. Treat them with respect and caution and at least you'd likely walk away.

The police department's Eighth Precinct was quite familiar with Sumner. Especially on that day in my freshman year when a near-riot occurred. When it was all over, two students had been wounded, though not seriously, by police gunfire. I remember milling with hundreds of other students watching cops wrestle with miscreants. In fact,

I wasn't ten feet away from a fracas that erupted as a cop tried to arrest a student. I remember the student pinning the cop and trying vainly to wrest his pistol from its holster. The cop's partner and an oaken nightstick helped subdue the student, without use of excessive force, given the circumstances.

The police made their presence known in other ways at Sumner, too. During my time there, the hallways once buzzed with the news that a student had been shot to death by police while allegedly robbing a store. The episode barely rated a mention in the briefs column of the local newspapers. A teacher discussing the matter in class shrugged resignedly and said the late Sumnerite was a thug who'd come to a likely end.

The duality of black life, with the police playing the roles of both savior and oppressor, was also evident at Sumner. I remember when a couple of students were arrested in connection with a robbery that left a store clerk dead. The Monday following the murder, one of the suspects was back in school, telling folks that "they had to let us go for lack of evidence."

My Professional Life

My work as a journalist has heavily influenced my views about crime perpetrated against the black community, both from without and from within. I spent my early years as a reporter writing about police and court news. That meant I often worked out of an office at police headquarters or the county courts.

Most mornings, as I settled into my courthouse office, I was treated to a powerful passion play showing what one facet of slavery must have been like. You could hear it before you saw it—a low, rhythmic, metallic clank punctuated by the murmur of voices. Then came the footsteps, gradually growing louder. Even with my back to the door, I could tell by the sound that another group of jail inmates was

being led into the courthouse. Eventually, a group of men would shuffle past my open door. Yes, shuffle. You can't do much else when you're
shackled by leg irons and handcuffs and linked to your jailmates by a
common "belly chain." Sometimes the men's voices were animated,
sometimes resigned, often angry, rarely reflective or sad. Sometimes
they spoke harshly about the system that had snared them; others
joked about the trip to the penitentiary while holding cardboard boxes
crammed with the regulation, twelve-inch-screen black-and-white
TVs and the few other personal items allowed them.

Each workday, I sat in on criminal trials and other judicial pro-
ceedings. I've watched at least a thousand people be judged by juries.
I've watched black prospective jurors give obviously wack answers during jury selection in hopes of eluding a place in that box with twelve
seats.

Given that roughly a half million white people have fled the city of
St. Louis, if you're a black person on trial there, chances are your jury
will include at least a few faces of color. If you're lucky, the jury may be
half black, or even mostly black.

Don't count on black jurors sparing you, though. The O.J.-like syn-
drome of exonerating an individual to strike a blow for the oppressed
collective didn't happen much, from what I saw. If you were good for the
crime—and I'd say 99 percent of the people I wrote about were guilty—
you'd better duck, as Ice Cube said, because the book was comin'.

I've watched black men and white men alike stand before the bar
of justice and be sentenced to society's ultimate penalty—death. Their
fate was intoned by both white male jurists and African-American
women who had become enough a part of the system to don black
robes and swing the gavel of justice.

During my years as a crime reporter, I wrote about varying degrees
of police brutality against both blacks and whites. The incidents
ranged from nonlethal blows delivered with a police-issue nightstick
to fatal shootings. In many cases, the violence was unjustified in my
mind. Sometimes the cops paid at least a token price for their mis-
deeds; in other instances, they escaped judicial penalties.

I also filed stories on a daily basis about black-on-black crime. In the city of St. Louis, when a crime's committed, chances are good that both assailant and victim are black. To me, that's the real tragedy: the great majority of crime against us is largely ignored by us, in favor of railing against the thankfully isolated instances of police shootings. Far more black people die by our own hands than are killed by those who wear a badge. We should be fighting harder to reduce, if not eliminate, those depressing statistics. Is changing us from within that much harder than attempting to change those outside our ranks? Ask the old folks: Poverty in our community hasn't always had a direct correlation with felonious violence.

In my work, I wrote too often about the senseless murders of cops, black and white, women and men killed trying to do a rough job for a largely ungrateful society. One lesson that helped me see another side of things was spending a morning with sheriff's deputies and an FBI instructor going through F.A.T.S., short for Firearms Simulation Training. With the aid of a large video monitor and a laser-firing pistol, the F.A.T.S. system tries to teach cops when and, more important, when not to drop the hammer on their weapons. Shoot, or don't shoot, that's the life-or-death discretion F.A.T.S. scenarios seek to instill in cops—rookies and veterans alike.

It's easy to get immersed in the video, which shows a cop's-eye view of routine patrols, traffic stops, and other situations cops encounter every day. In one event, for example, as I approached a car from the rear, I noticed the trunk slightly ajar. Before I completed that thought, the trunk popped open to reveal a shotgun-wielding assailant. Drawing the laser weapon, I fired several shots. The tape then stopped and text popped onto the screen outlining the number of shots fired and the elapsed time. In this case, it was less than two seconds from start to finish. Another scenario countdown indicated .364 of a second elapsed between the time the threat materialized and I fired a first shot. One-third of a second to decide life, or possible death. Snap your fingers fast once and it'll take about that long. One heartbeat's worth of time to assess a perceived threat and react. Make the right call and you go home that night; somebody else might not. Make the wrong call and you, the cop, might die. That's something to think about the next time you sit around for hours debating whether a cop made the right shoot/no-shoot decision in the real world.

By the way, I didn't survive F.A.T.S. My reflexes failed me when an elevator door opened to reveal gun-toting assassins who immediately opened fire on me and the diplomat I was supposedly guarding. I was dead before my hand could reach the laser pistol at my side.

Always a Hoodrat

Unlike many African-Americans who've scraped, cajoled, or ass-kissed their way into decent employment, I've never lived in the 'burbs. Admittedly, I once lived less than a hundred feet inside the city limits, which meant that I got the benefit of a suburban zip code but could still cast my ballot for a largely black electoral slate and retain the moral superiority to occasionally tongue-lash those who'd fled the 'hood.

Besides paying twice as much as need be for car insurance, living in the city has other drawbacks as well as advantages, such as a much shorter commute to work. I became a homeowner in 1991. That changed my perspective toward the police and crime, both immediately and in incremental ways over time. Once I signed on the dotted line, I had a six-figure investment riding both on the 5,500 square feet of Planet Earth that now belonged to me and the finance company, as well as the neighborhood around it.

I've come up with a theory that black folks often buy houses, while white folks usually buy neighborhoods. That's true in my case because when I bought a home I ignored the huge Section 8 apartment building that looms over my backyard. Not to mention the mental hospital that was under construction nearby. Not exactly a place to count on property values outrunning inflation. Since America doesn't have kibbutzes, I believe I'm entitled to make money on my home's price appreciation, just like your average suburbanite. If the police can help maintain my investment and my safety, I've got no problem dialing 911—and have done so a few times.

I used to wonder why white people, at least those smart enough to think about it, fought so hard to fortify their neighborhoods against crime and decay. Now I know why. The trouble with white America's dysfunctional logic is it too often equates those maladies with black people. I understood at least part of their motivation, if not the underlying racism, once I got a tax bill showing that the value of my real estate had dropped, this during a booming economy.

Part of the reason my home is lagging in value is that it's just north of an imaginary dividing line in St. Louis that is the border between black and white, between perceived safety and the myth of wild lawlessness. The truth, as usual, is somewhere in between. Still, if you think perception's not reality, dream on; my home appraisal settles the debate for me.

"It's black people like you who're the problem!"

I've become a lot more territorial since buying a home. The property is mine. I bought it, I pay taxes on it, and I don't take lightly those who trespass upon it. From time to time, I've had run-ins with the brethren who've occasionally chosen to cross me at home. Apparently, a sizable number of our people take a more communal view of home and property: If I see it, I can steal it and, gee whiz, I wonder why this Uncle Tom negro's chasing me down the street.

More than once, I've told a brother—nicely at first—not to sit on my front steps, whistle at his drug supplier from my driveway, cut through my backyard, or even not to steal the newspaper off my lawn. The usual response is incredulousness at the notion that a black man actually owns something worth maintaining, followed by belligerent threats. My late grandmother's old warning to me still holds true for them: "Don't let your mouth overload your ass."

So far, no violence has broken out, but there have been a few near misses. Twice, black men have pulled onto our usually quiet street to whip their girlfriends. In one instance, the assailant threatened my next-door neighbor with a pistol when my neighbor tried to intervene. In the second case, the police answered our calls in time to arrest the man, but the woman declined to prosecute. A few weeks later, I saw them walking down the street, arm in arm, two crackheads together again.

In another incident, the same neighbor's son—a frat brother of mine—was boldly threatened by a black male who pulled into his driveway, almost to the front door, then blew his horn repeatedly in the middle of the night, likely a signal for the drug runners who regularly infest the Section 8 palace close by. "Muthaf******, you might get hurt" was his reply when asked to move on. He'll probably never know that had he made any sudden, threatening moves, one, possibly two of the homeowners around his car were prepared for his sorry ass.

If it sounds like the Wild West, in a way it is. As Fannie Lou Hamer once said, you get sick and tired of being sick and tired. In the twenty-first century, your own people can be as much a threat to you as Jim Crow ever was. Despite all the loud protestations by so-called black leaders for more gun control as a solution to crime, most black folks I know who live in the 'hood have a little "somethin'-somethin' " tucked away for emergencies, gun laws be damned. That's a strong testament to the depraved state of our current existence.

The Passage of Time

As I close in on age forty, the "youth of old age," I sometimes wonder why the police—so far—don't hassle me much anymore. On the rare occasions when I do get stopped for running a red light or something, the cops are likely to call me "sir." I'm not naive enough to think all is well, though. I still follow the black man's survival rules for police encounters. So far, they've kept me alive.

Still, I wonder, is my relative freedom from police harassment due to my advancing age—am I now too old to match the profile? Are cops better trained these days in terms of dealing with issues of color? Or is

America changing almost two generations after Rev. Martin Luther King's death? Are today's young white cops more comfortable with black people thanks to cross-cultural media images, integrated schools, music videos, and the like? Does this slight melding of America's disparate cultures mean young police officers are bringing less racial baggage to work? I hope so. Only time will tell.

What Do I Tell My Fast-Growing Son

As I get older, I don't worry so much about me. I do worry about my eight-year-old son. When he stands at the edge of manhood, will the same survival rules still apply? I pray not; let's hope the world will have moved on by then.

I'll pass down the rules anyway—at heart, I don't have much faith in the world's ability to change. I wonder, though, will my hardheaded boy who's growing up in a seemingly integrated America even listen? Will his experiences at a school that values diversity blind him to the dangers of the real world?

I remember hearing an older fraternity brother worry aloud about the safety of his son as he sat at a bar several years ago. "I tell him don't ride with no white girls and don't have a whole carload of young bucks in your car, either," he told another brother.

Makes a world of sense to me. I'll repeat that advice to my boy soon—too soon.

MEDIATION IN BLACK
AND WHITE

Unequal Distribution of Empowerment by Police

CHRISTOPHER COOPER

Often, when police go into black communities they do not
empower people—rather they dictate to them. It should be of grave
concern to black people that as we speak there is a movement afoot,
comprised predominantly of people not of color, that vigorously
opposes police empowering people of color. This same movement
has remained silent on the ongoing practice, since the beginning of
modern policing in the United States, of police officers empowering white people.

In a *Saturday Review* article published soon after the Watts riots, a
writer observed, "It is inconceivable that the police treat the people of
Watts with the same attitudes and methods as those they apply to the
middle-class white community."[1] This inequality of policing styles,
one for blacks (and other visible minorities, specifically Latinos) and

---

[1] Murray L. Schwartz, "Beyond the Los Angeles Riots: A Hard Lesson for the
Law." *Saturday Review* 48 (Nov. 13, 1965) 35.

another for whites, is still a ubiquitous mark on the national landscape. The resulting social injustice is profoundly evident in the manner in which many white police officers (and even some black officers) respond to nonviolent and non-law-breaking interpersonal disputes involving black people.

When whites are involved in a non-law-breaking interpersonal dispute that prompts police attention, overwhelmingly, police officers empower the disputants to help themselves. Put another way, the police officers *mediate*. Mediation is a conflict-resolution methodology that dates back approximately three thousand years. It is characterized as a neutral third party helping others to resolve an interpersonal dispute. Most significant about the process is the fact that the parties involved in the dispute fashion their own resolution—the course of action is determined by them, not by the third party. The mediator is the skilled facilitator—his/her role is only to assist. He or she does not make the resolution or impose a decision. In the context of policing, mediation would involve an officer coming into your home, place of business, or personal space and transferring decision-making power to you and the other person so that the two of you could empower yourselves.

This is a dignified and respectful police response that officers seldom—if ever—provide to people of color. This is a response that human beings deserve, yet many police officers will not transfer decision-making power in interpersonal disputes when the parties in dispute are black. Officers either dictate the resolution or conduct an inept form of arbitration.

I am a black man in America who became a "black cop" in America. When some black officers put on a police uniform, they become obstacles to the desired end of equal policing, but not once did I ever forget who I was and what I stood for. I knew that because of my skin color the policing establishment would never let me become a "full-fledged member" of the police subculture—not a problem, since I never wanted any type of membership. This is a subculture of weapons planting, unlawful shooting, and adhering to a premeditated script that justifies every outrageous police action—a subculture that has wreaked havoc on black people since the dawn of policing in the United States.

Conflict and dispute are normal. All human beings experience this inevitable fact of life. In many ways the conflicts and disputes in which we play a role as a party (disputant) are helpful, since they can lead to clarity, understanding, personal growth, and societal change. Regardless of the community, police officers assigned to patrol duties are tasked with responding to interpersonal disputes. The uniformed patrol officer, unlike other types of police officers, is the first responder to many such disputes. Many of these kinds of conflicts are addressed by the patrol officer where they occur: in disputants'/parties' homes, offices, on street corners, in shopping malls, on basketball courts, and in parking lots, just to name a few places. Sometimes the officer is summoned; in other cases, he/she comes upon a dispute in progress.

Examples of disputes that prompt a police intervention include neighbor disputes such as conflicts over driveway access and on-street parking; customer-merchant disputes; (portable) property disputes (e.g., televisions and clothing); and roommate disputes. Some of the disputes to which the patrol officer responds are marked by flared tempers and/or chaos, while others are orderly.

Many interpersonal disputes to which the police respond are not ongoing. I call these types of disputes episodic. An example of an episodic dispute is a customer-merchant (e.g., street or flea market vendor) dispute in which a customer desires an exchange or refund of an item and the merchant refuses. Mall parking-space squabbles are another example. These are situations in which the parties will not have reason to see each other again. Other disputes that officers encounter have a history or are ongoing. Both types of disputes are always ripe for intervention by highly skilled police officers trained in mediation.

Upon the police officer's arrival at an interpersonal dispute, he/she has the authority to determine what kind of problem-solving strategy should be employed. The police patrol toolbox of responses includes mediation, threats/coercion, and arrest. The officer might also dictate to or order the disputants, with or without arbitration. All of these methodologies have a time and place for use.

The option of arbitration involves the police officer giving each party an opportunity to explain his/her side and, based on the facts presented, rendering a decision. There are situations in which arbitration may be appropriate, for example, cases in which there is absolutely no doubt that a piece of property belongs to another. If I were to strike you over the head and take your Walkman, not only would I be guilty of battery, but I also would have created a dispute. The dispute is suited for arbitration, since upon examination of the facts, it will become clear that I am not entitled to the property. The Walkman belongs to you. The officer has the legitimate right to order me to return your Walkman (in addition, the officer can arrest me). Many interpersonal disputes in society are not so cut-and-dry. Often, both parties/disputants have a legitimate claim to the (identical) outcome sought by the other. Since identical outcomes for each party are not always feasible, it is through collective and integrative problem-solving (mediation) that parties often compromise.

Most mediated agreements are compromises. For this reason, mediation is a preferred conflict-resolution method, since the parties get to have control over the contents of the agreement—they make the agreement themselves. In this way, both parties walk away from the process winners and with dignity intact, although they may walk away with less than what they originally sought.

Contrasting Mediation with Ordering and Arbitration

Many interpersonal disputes to which the police respond are suited for an agreement arrived at solely by the parties (the officer would only be a facilitator). Therefore, when the disagreement or dispute is better suited to mediation, there is a lot inherently wrong when the officer instead dictates how the matter will be resolved. It is common knowledge to black and many Latino people that, too often, disputes between people of color that are suitable for mediation are handled by police officers through dictatorial control (or authoritarianism coupled with threats of what would be an unlawful arrest) and intentionally inept arbitration. Because neither dictating nor arbitration is warranted in such instances, the police officers demonstrate considerable disrespect for the parties' legitimate expectation to be involved in resolving their own problem.

Inappropriate use of arbitration by police is a serious problem in black communities, either when used for a matter that was amenable to mediation or when arbitration was warranted but performed haphazardly by the officer involved. For example, the officer does not give both parties an opportunity to present their case or the officer does not base his/her decision on the facts. Essentially, it is an officer showing indifference or lack of interest in the matter for which the citizens have sought police assistance. A typical result involves the officer directing the transfer of property to one party or the other when both parties have an equal right to possession. Put bluntly, it is an officer coming into your home or your personal space and dictating how you will resolve an issue that you have every right to participate in resolving.

Just as bad, in many interpersonal disputes to which the police respond in black communities, police dictating and arbitration are marked by police use of profanity and a pronounced lack of civility. The worst-case scenarios are those in which the officers address the interpersonal dispute (e.g., a dispute between neighbors regarding a barking dog) via brutality and/or making an unlawful arrest.

Another example of the general inequality in police responses between blacks and whites occurred one early morning in Washington, D.C., when I was on duty. A large contingent of police officers, myself included, was assigned to a detail—a name for something not typical, such as a special event, and often not in the area where an officer is permanently assigned. The detail was in downtown Washington, in the heart of the business center, shopping district, and tourist area. This was in contrast to my being a cop permanently assigned to the "other" D.C., the D.C. that tourists don't see. My police district/precinct contained many predominantly black neighborhoods in which poverty, human suffering, and the sounds of gunshots were frequent occurrences.

As you will see, many "details" meant that cultural and environmental adaptations were imposed on us. On this morning, five officers crammed into a police car. There was one other black officer present. The driver was a white sergeant, higher in rank than all of us. He wasted no time in barking out orders. He told us we were going to help maintain crowd control at an event at which Russian president Mikhail Gorbachev would pass by in a motorcade and wave to onlookers—a parade of sorts. The onlookers who lined block after block, we would later see, were predominantly white, many of them tourists. As the sergeant drove us to the event, he shouted, "Now you're going downtown, there are no 'motherfuckas' or 'yo's' down there—it's 'sir,' 'ma'am,' 'please,' 'thank you,' 'excuse me.' " He told us how we would have to take concerns and requests from onlookers seriously. I kept silent, but my anger built. I was angry that it was okay according to this sergeant, and so many others, for the police to address people in my community with profanity and a lack of interest. Fortunately, there were many officers like myself who did not address people with profanity. We spoke to all people with respect and took their concerns seriously.

Now, let us return to our discussion of mediation. Critics might be quick to inquire why disputants would summon the police if they wanted to empower themselves. The response is twofold. First, the disputants do not always call the police—sometimes someone else calls the police, not necessarily because the situation is volatile, but perhaps because it is "loud." At other times, officers come upon a dispute in progress. Still, there are those cases in which disputing parties summon the police. It is a natural and sensible action, since third-party intervenors offer many benefits in helping others resolve their interpersonal disputes. Even the best of us are involved in disputes in which we recognize that negotiation (a process that does not involve a third-party intervenor but one in which the parties in dispute are the only people present) will not work. We realize that the third-party intervenor can help us identify the issues, recognize common ground, and administer a goal-directed resolution process. Dictating (or ordering and arbitration), when not warranted, represents a style of policing that alienates community members and rightly fuels a negative perception of police by people of color.

Examining Why Mediation Is Not Afforded to People of Color

In order to put the relevant issues into context, note that mediation is indigenous to police work, yet very few American police officers have been given formal instruction on how exactly to do it. Because of the nature of patrol police work, for many police officers, learning to mediate is a naturally occurring problem-solving technique. As a result, many patrol police officers mediate anyway (although many do so only selectively). Granted, the absence of formal mediation instruction indicates that the employment of the method is not always systematic or the most competent. Nonetheless, there are police officers who are high quality mediators even without training, because they came to the profession with excellent social skills and a commitment to treat people with dignity.

Unfortunately, many people hired as police officers possess below-standard social-interaction skills. For this reason alone, they should have been disqualified from employment as a police officer. Notwithstanding this fact, many officers often arrive at using mediation through trial-and-error and/or socialization. The former represents a patrol police officer arriving at a point, after responding to countless interpersonal disputes, at which he realizes what works, what does not work, and what is efficient. In particular, the officer realizes that there are benefits in transferring decision-making power to the parties/disputants. For example, he notices the enormous staying power of mediated agreements—they last because parties have a sense of ownership of them (because they created them). The officer contrasts this finding/observation with knowledge that an agreement resulting from arbitration, for example, is not as likely to last—a reflection of the old adage that no one likes being told what to do.

The officer's newfound solution (mediation) can imply that he/she is suddenly adorned with the social graces that are the mark of a respectful cop, but not necessarily. On the other hand, it more likely means that he/she has figured out how to expedite matters. So the officer's motivation to use the method may or may not reflect a desire to show respect to citizens. For some officers, mediation represents the best way to expedite matters that they consider an annoyance. They want to reduce the likelihood of a repeat call, thereby having the time to engage in other nonpolice activity (e.g., sleep.) or police activity that they find more interesting. Other officers may have similar motives but may also derive satisfaction from transferring power and showing respect for the citizens' rights to play a role in resolving their own disputes.

In addition to learning via trial and error, the socialization process plays a role in the adoption of mediation as a technique. It sometimes occurs via institutional compulsion, in which an officer has been taught or compelled to provide automatic deference to white disputants. In such situations, police officers usually transfer decision-making power to these individuals as a matter of course. For example, an officer may ask white disputants how the police can help them (the disputants) help themselves. The officer becomes an active, assertive facilitator as he helps the disputants find common ground. Additionally, he participates in brainstorming, not to coerce or impose but to help the disputants realize alternatives to resolving the matter that they may not have considered. Such scenarios illustrate the social inequalities inherent in police responses. Consider the findings of a research effort by two white researchers who studied approximately five thousand police responses to interpersonal disputes in American cities. They found that patrol police officers would work closely with disputing parties of higher socioeconomic class (almost all of whom were white) "to help them identify alternatives to resolving their dispute." But officers would not provide the same service to lower-class parties, almost all of whom were people of color.[2]

Other officers may use mediation selectively—for example, they provide it for whites, but not for blacks or identifiable Latinos. Blame for selective use of mediation should be laid equally on the individual officer as well as the police department that employs him. The reason: unlike the examples of institutional socialization discussed above, an officer is a free agent; he is able to follow his own propensity to behave in a racially discriminatory manner. The department is culpable because it encourages and condones racially discriminatory behavior by an officer.

The close-minded officer asserts that his avoidance of or dictatorial role in addressing interpersonal disputes in communities is based on his notion that blacks and Latinos are, by nature, violence-prone. Perversely, he maintains that since people of color (in his mind) prefer using violence to solve their own disputes, they will not object to the police using a similar approach.

Consider a white Boston police officer's view regarding use of mediation in a community of color in that city. He wrote the following in a term paper for a 1999 university course examining police use of mediation: "I am not a racist nor do I feel I discriminate against certain races or religions. I will say, though, the Haitian culture along with the Latino culture has a propensity for shall we say, getting a little hot under the collar. It's hard enough just trying to keep them separated, never mind trying to explain to them some sort of ground rules that we want them to follow." In the final sentence, the officer is referring to the ground rules of the mediation process.

The officer's assertion and the theme of his entire paper show that

---

[2] Smith and Klein, "Police Control of Interpersonal Disputes," *Social Problems* 31:4 (1984): 468–81.

he is saying that because of what he believes are Haitian and Latino propensities, the parties do not possess the requisite civil, emotional, or intellectual capacity for handling empowerment. The officer added that his former partner "had the patience of a Saint" and would "stand in somebody's living room or out in a courtyard of the projects" and empower/mediate people to help themselves. In contrast to his partner, he argued that "locking" people up for being involved in interpersonal disputes made more sense. He said: "I had almost as much success as my partner . . . and in a lot less time."[3]

The Movement Opposing Mediation by Police

Many current police-mediation center partnerships perpetuate the reliance on unlawful arrest, unnecessary arbitration, and avoidance, which is commonplace in communities of color. In the administration of justice, people of color suffer the most when the police fail to take proper action.

In interpersonal dispute situations to which the police respond, where the police have no grounds to arrest or cite for a violation of law, and in which the matters in contention are not clear-cut, mediation by the police usually makes sense. However, in some U.S. jurisdictions, there are actually efforts to keep police officers from mediating in communities of color. Leading the efforts are people who are members of the mediation profession and are best described as conflict resolution professionals. Most of these people are not of color and they represent mediation organizations. The organizations are usually not-for-profit, but making money to keep the centers in business is a major objective. One such strategy involves partnering with police agencies in order that police refer disputing citizens to the mediation centers. The

---

[3] For legal reasons, the officer must not be identified.

steady stream of referrals from the police means that the mediation center is eligible for grant monies or direct payment for each case that it mediates. So at the request of the mediation center and pursuant to the partnership agreement, when police are called to an interpersonal dispute that is amenable to mediation, the officers are to refer the disputing parties to a mediation center. In many cases, the officers are provided with referral forms. Additionally, officers may take the information of the parties and pass it on to the mediation center. The mediation center, in turn, usually in a few days following the dispute, notifies the parties that their presence is requested at mediation.[4]

The problem with this type of police-mediation partnership is that officers can only hand out referral slips, rather than provide the disputants with the mediation option that is needed at that time. Although mediation centers do not have the authority to prohibit officers from mediating, centers strongly suggest that officers refrain from mediating. To reduce the likelihood that officers will mediate, the mediation centers intentionally neglect to provide officers with the training they need to perfect their mediation skills. Police–mediation center partnerships of this type are usually targeted at communities of color and such communities often have an existent problem of inadequate police responses. In this way, the mediation centers are reinforcing officers' tendency to avoid employing the deferential responses that they typically provide to white disputants.

Yes, the existence of a community-based mediation center coupled with a police referral process is laudable. Before the advent of mediation centers, if police referred at all, they referred people to the courts. It is in everyone's best interest that U.S. society become less litigious and more inclined to use mediation. But the process is discriminatory and degrading if it prohibits cops from offering to mediate where it is most needed: on the scene. The referral option should always be pre-

---

[4]The National Association for Community Mediation's website lists mediation centers in forty-three states and the District of Columbia.

sent, since the officer may not be able to mediate the underlying issues of the dispute: the issues may be so involved that they require the kind of extended attention that a mediation center could offer. For this reason, it makes sense that, after the officer has done his "substantive" part, if necessary, he make a referral. A police department–mediation partnership of this sort is one that provides for substantive handling of interpersonal disputes, in a dignified manner. Those mediation professionals who are opposed to police mediating but enthusiastic about cops functioning as mere referral agents should ask themselves the following question: If the police do not empower citizens when empowerment is called for, then what is it that the police will do? The answer: Leave disputants with a stern warning (deriving from the arbitration and dictation techniques discussed earlier) along with referral forms to the mediation center. The response is no different from the way things were done before mediation center–police department partnerships, except that now the parties are also given a piece of paper (referral form). This superficial response, like putting a Band-Aid on a severed artery, can jeopardize the safety of people of color. Once the police leave, the dispute may grow considerably worse and become violent. This is one of the most important reasons why officers have a moral duty to treat "scenes" in a substantive manner. They would be negligent in their duty if they did not. Moreover, in many situations, the mere sight and distribution of referral cards will not cause many disputants to cease expressing themselves to the police or another party—the police must do more.

This issue brings to mind a call to which I and several other officers responded. It was in a high-rise building in a poverty-stricken black community in Washington. The elevators were broken as usual, so approximately five other officers and I climbed seven flights of stairs. Upon our arrival, we encountered a chaotic situation. It was neighbor against neighbor. About fifteen people were arguing loudly in the narrow hallway. The tenants had taken sides and were physically "facing off." Punches had been thrown and people were both angry and emotional. My partner and I began the mediation process. It was going well when I received a call on my radio from a police supervisor. I was told to have all units, myself included, leave the building. The supervisor said, "Let them kill each other and we'll pick up the pieces later." We had no choice but to leave. I have not forgotten that night. The order to leave was another typical example of the marginalization of black people's self-worth, and the deprivation of citizens' right to a substantive and deferential police response. In this regard, I doubt the commitment to racial equality of many of my colleagues in the mediation field, since they oppose cops making substantive attempts to address interpersonal disputes.

Granted, the problem of overuse of arbitration and dictation by the police is a dilemma for which the police institution is largely to blame; however, mediation centers should not use this fact as a scapegoat to explain away its complicity in perpetuating the practice of superficial and dictatorial police responses. By encouraging officers not to empower citizens, the centers are implying that all alternatives (except mediation), such as arbitration, dictation, unlawful threats and arrest, and even unlawful force, are appropriate. Mediation centers must not stand in the way of officers doing something more substantive than the above responses. And any substantive action must respect citizens and allow for their dignity to remain intact.

An Examination of Motivations

Among reasons given by some mediation professionals for their opposition to police mediating is that, in their opinion, police officers are unable to remain neutral since they represent the criminal justice system. Obviously, this is not a sensible argument. The officer is capable of not taking sides on the scene. Just as a judge who also works for the government has taken an oath to remain neutral, so can a police officer. Note that the same people who argue against cops empowering people do not oppose judges adjudicating, although there should be great concern that some judges do not hold to their oath of neutrality.

The real reasons for opposition to police empowering people (in particular people of color) are greed, racism, classism, and privilege. Greed motivates some mediation centers, particularly those that have entered into agreements with police and are therefore concerned with increasing their own profits (they are often paid a fee for each case referred). Nonprofit centers also stand to gain by showing their funding sources that continued funding is justified. Center operators fear that if police officers mediate interpersonal disputes "on the scene," the referral caseload will decrease. It is difficult to comprehend their position when a common mission of a mediation organization is that of spreading to as many people as possible the notion that there are better alternatives (e.g., mediation) to violence and litigation. There is enough conflict to go around. The mediation center is not likely to become bankrupt if officers empower citizens. Moreover, in the case of episodic disputes (e.g., dispute over a mall parking space that does not have underlying issues), it would be ludicrous for an officer to make a referral to a mediation center.

Racism and classism are factors that influence police officers to show heightened respect for white people. It is known that police officers do transfer decision-making power to white people. So there is deference paid to white people—a respect for a white citizen's expectation that he/she has a say in how a dispute in which he/she is involved is resolved. Many white people have a vested interest in not seeing this practice change; hence they will block police officers' attempts to use mediation in communities of color.

A person's privileged status in society also influences opposition to police officers mediating because it stands in the way of a person realizing that: (1) mediation is indigenous to police work, an indelible imprint on the profession; (2) mediation has been afforded to white people since the beginning of modern policing; (3) mediation is selectively used by many police officers; and (4) police officers have a duty to provide substantive police responses that show respect and allow a citizen to keep his or her dignity.

Having had some interaction with police helps to know what officers do when they intervene in a dispute. Because of their privileged status, many whites have never had such an experience. Rather, the extent of their interaction with police officers is either pursuant to a traffic infraction or their seeking directions. On the other hand, black people are constantly subjected to unwarranted police attention. When we, especially males, have a disagreement with a white store clerk, airline ticket agent, or movie house attendant, for example, it is not uncommon that the police are called "on us." The caller describes us as a "disorderly person" or as "creating a disturbance." We are described by the clerk, etc., as having been aggressive in our mannerisms or that our physical size is intimidating—I have heard both allegations about me from countless customer service agents with which I have had a disagreement. When the typical white police officer arrives, he almost always defers to the white person. When a white person has a disagreement with a customer service provider, the phenomenon is described as a "difference of opinion" that does not require a police response. If the police were to respond, they would mediate. Contrast this with black people knowing too well the phenomenon of being maced or dragged off to jail for having been involved in an interpersonal dispute with a white person. My mother always told me that because I was black, I could not do some of the things that are legal even though white people do them, because if I do those same things, I will be treated as if I have done something illegal. Mediation professionals have a responsibility to address relations between police and people of color. In their partnerships with police departments, mediation centers should not implement any programs that fail to push for equitable and dignified police services for everyone.

Conclusion

Poor relations, in particular between people of color and police, are at epidemic levels throughout the United States. The relationship is strained in part by police arbitrating and dictating in situations in which citizens have a legitimate expectation that they should be empowered to help themselves.

The fact that police departments throughout the country have been involved in behavior that suggests that many of their officers would be unwilling to treat black people fairly does not mean that officers should not be compelled to perform their duty. Rather, communities of color should vigorously challenge racially discriminatory policing in all its forms. Many whites have a vested interest in keeping black people socially subordinate. One way of accomplishing their goal is to influence police policy and stand in the way of police empowering people of color.

Finally, a mediation center–police department partnership should have moral, humane, and socially conscious objectives. Such objectives would have to call for humanitarian actions by mediation centers and ensure that all members of the respective community are treated with dignity and respect. A strategy that encourages officers to merely refer parties to a mediation center does not accomplish these objectives. Morally proper police responses are those that are substantive and not preferential.

"Details" often encroach on the moral values of officers like myself. The "there are no motherfuckas [*sic*] here" order, along with similar statements, supports a notion that people should be treated equally regardless of social class, neighborhood, or race. In this regard, I end by describing a day when I was one of many black officers assigned to safeguard the Ku Klux Klan as it marched for white supremacy on Washington, D.C., streets. On command we took up positions on a riot line. There were hundreds of us, standing in row after row spread across Pennsylvania Avenue, poised in an attack stance. We had guns, batons, pepper spray, and gas masks and were dressed in full riot gear, helmets and all. Our brothers and sisters threw bottles and cans at us. They stood within several feet of our bodies, looked intensely through our glass helmet shields covering our faces and into our eyes, and repeatedly came within several inches of our faces. Then, with rage, the black crowd called us "house niggers" who "worked for the man!" I only wished they could have seen more through our helmets—they would have realized that we didn't want to be there. They would have realized that many of those helmet-covered black faces, and some white as well, recognized their duty to offer the same level of policing services, specifically, empowerment, to our people that is afforded to most white people.

WHAT I LEARNED
IN SCHOOL

MAT JOHNSON

I've never gotten upset about the way black men are treated by the American justice system because I've never had any faith in the people in power in the first place. I don't trust the ability of the larger white society to see us clearly, without all of the social connotations that accompany our ethnicity, whether they be cops, judges, or reporters. To me, the white justice system appears to be just another erratic destructive force in life best avoided, like tornadoes. No matter how many bills are passed or protests made, interpreting law still comes down to individual perspective, and that's where we get screwed. Debating the validity of the inhumane treatment of victims such as Dorismond and Diallo can sometimes seem like arguing about the fairness of the mud slides in Mexico.

But there is a code of conduct, a system of social law and justice I'm ruled by every day. I'm fascinated with it, mostly because I rarely understand it. It's the one we black Americans have created for ourselves. It's the one that binds the place in which I now live, Harlem, as well as the place I grew up in, northwest Philadelphia.

Given this interest, when I heard about a book called *Code of the*

Street, a sociological study of the very Philadelphia area I grew up in, I knew I had to pick it up. Using Germantown Avenue, a historic road that passes from one of Philadelphia's most affluent areas to its poorest, as a metaphor, Elijah Anderson examines the difference between what he identifies as "decent" culture, which applies to the majority of people in the neighborhood, people invested in the goals of the larger society, and the minority culture of violence and poverty called "street" culture. He also explores how both groups survive together in communities where the law seems to be imposed by an absentee, uncaring world. In decent culture, people follow the rules and try to get ahead, basing their self-worth and dreams on the ideals reinforced by the larger society. In street culture, there is a lack of faith in the larger society, its goals and possibilities, so that the law itself becomes something to be avoided. In this world, the more aggressive street culture rules, and violence is the key to the food chain.

This portrait of society in *Code of the Street* was so familiar, so rational, so simple that I couldn't put the book down until there were no more words to hold me. It made sense of an environment that I often have found chaotic and arbitrary. As I was reading this book, what shocked me the most about this model was how accurately I could apply it to another environment I experienced when growing up, one that greatly impacted how I now view the entire world. That place was Henry H. Houston Elementary, my grade school.

I started my academic career at private school. At Green Street Friends there were, on average, eighteen kids to a class, and the teachers were involved, attentive, and caring. Set within a Victorian schoolhouse of classic wooden moldings, tall ceilings, and large, airy windows, the environment was as relaxed as an inner-city elementary school could be. My kindergarten and first-grade classes were near evenly divided in numbers between black and white, much like the city we lived in. Because it was a Quaker institution, the faculty and staff worked to create an environment of nonviolence and racial harmony. Despite the fact that half my class was white, we spent much of first grade learning about the history of Africa. The only act of violence I can remember from my time there was when I pushed a kid at recess for torturing a spider. For this I was immediately removed from the school yard and lectured. When I got home, my parents had already received a call about the incident. The next day I came in with my homework, an apology card I'd made out of construction paper and Elmer's. Green Street was everything you could imagine a school could or should be, a bastion of the decent, middle-class life. But then my dad ran out of money and I got sent to Houston.

If I'd been a little older, I would have spent the whole summer wetting my bed and trying to learn judo. Instead, I didn't even get nervous about the experience until my dad brought me to school the first day. The registration office was filled with fat ladies attached to swivel chairs who yelled at us and each other. There was no line to get their attention, just a mob that nearly pushed over the front desk. I had never seen adults act this way. It was my first encounter with "government" as a somewhat hostile, ineffectual beast, but it was an impression that stayed with me for the rest of my life. If my father could have heard me over the yelling, I would have told him it wasn't worth it, I could remain illiterate, or maybe we could put some real education on layaway. Getting service in this place was not about fairness or order, but about how loud you could scream.

Shaken, we headed to the yard where I was supposed to meet my class. Actually, to call it a yard is misleading—except in the prison sense of the word—since it was just one huge slab of empty concrete, a parking lot no cars had bothered to sit on. Following the numbers spray-painted to ground, we found my class of thirty-six kids standing in a row. When the teacher came by and slapped the kid in front of me hard enough to knock him out of line, I immediately realized the age of educational benevolence was over.

A week into this intense experience, I learned words from the other kids to put my situation in more succinct terms: I was fucked. By Halloween I not only knew the Holy Trinity of curses—shit, damn, and fuck—I knew what they *meant*. Unfortunately, that was the only way in which my vocabulary had improved. Not only were the books in my class under my reading level, out-of-date, and missing pages, some of the kids couldn't even read those.

We all knew who couldn't read. It was one of those innate things kids divine, like in nursery school when you could tell which kids were biters. The slow readers would stand up before the class, mortified, and painfully stumble through syllables, but no one would laugh because they were invariably the toughest kids in the school. Toughest is not a good description; it implies that they were kids like everyone else, just a little gruffer, like the bullies on 1950s TV shows. These kids, however, were a completely different species. Even in second grade, it was already clear that Houston was just the first gray cinder-block institution of many for them, the start of a long line that would eventually end with prison. They weren't there to grow academically: often they didn't even show up for class, choosing instead to roam the halls. They were completely uninvested in the system in which they found themselves, giving little thought to their futures.

Coming from a decent family, I had never been exposed to people not interested in "doing the right thing." Instead they only cared about doing the easiest thing, whatever they felt like doing right then, regardless of how it affected themselves or others. If you had something they wanted, a cool Snoopy pencil, a new Sixers hat, sneakers, whatever, they would take it from you right there, the moment they had the urge. Your tears would just fulfill their fantasies of omnipotence. They didn't care if you told on them; disciplinary actions against them were largely futile. Just as on the street, where incarceration can strengthen a street-oriented person's credibility, confidence, and criminal bent, flunking only made these students more powerful. Flunking meant that next year they would be even bigger and stronger than their new classmates. There were some of this species in every class, in every grade, and they all knew each other like they were one big fraternity. Some of them were related and those were the most dangerous ones because their influence passed beyond age barriers. Having an older brother who was a thug was the equivalent of being connected to the mob.

In my class, Tarrence Green was a gangland unto himself. Large, violent, and nearly illiterate, he had been known to attack older kids on little provocation and leave them crying and discredited. He was kind of our anti-Superboy, capable of inhuman feats and always on the scene whenever trouble erupted. And as Superboy had Krypto, Tarrence had his own dog mascot, Bitch, a male dog that had had its testicles nearly bit off in a fight so that they hung halfway down his leg. In class, I avoided Tarrence with the same extreme caution I would use when approaching a roof ledge on a tall building. Unfortunately, our classroom was only twenty feet by thirty feet.

My first moment of inevitable contact came in class, during an academic exercise. We were playing a game. The teacher would ask a question and whoever got it right would have the option of choosing the next raised hand to answer. Correct answers meant you could go to recess early. The questions were a breeze too. Everybody wanted in on it, including me, but due to the clannish loyalty built into elementary school social structure, it took what seemed like hours before someone of my lowly popularity got picked. By that time recess had already started and there was nobody left but the nerds—my friends—and the people who beat us up—the bullies—who being a slow breed had taken a while to figure out that the questions would barely stump a five-year-old. Finally, I got picked by the last vestige of the popular crowd on his way out the door, and my friends sighed in relief. Now it was our turn to play favorites. We would be running away from our desks in no time.

"Who can show me which hand is their left?" Mrs. Alexander asked, a little too eager to go on break. Across the room hands shot in the air once more. Jeremy Halpern, a chubby, halitosis-plagued boy with gray bags under his eyes, started smiling. He knew he was next. Jeremy wasn't my best friend, but he'd invited me to his birthday party the week before and now I was morally obligated. I had my finger pointed at him, was about to say his name, when I noticed Tarrence behind him. Tarrence was hanging over his desk, his right hand thrust forward so far it seemed only moments before he came crashing to the floor.

"Pick me or I'ma kick your ass at recess."

For a boy with normal hearing, it's amazing how easily I seemed to lip-read. I like to think now, twenty years later, that I paused before making my decision, that I bravely agonized over my choice.

"Tarrence Green."

But I didn't. I just, in that moment, got the best lesson I had had so far. That life was about swallowing your pride, biding your time, and covering the only ass God gave you. Our school was nominally run by the principal but it was really run by violence. Without ever hearing of Darwin, the kids had set up a classic "survival of the fittest" society, and nowhere was this more evident than out on the yard. The recess supervisors were at best clueless, at worst indifferent. Poorly educated women in their fifties and sixties, they simply didn't have enough energy to keep control of the chaos around them. Not that there weren't adults who could inspire fear in the most lumpen among us. There were enforcers—a gym teacher, the math guy—who were known and respected for their propensity for violence. The most notable was our principal, Mr. Davidson, a large, blubbery man called Mr. Walrus when he was far out of earshot. His weapon was the yard-stick. Once, after I heard a group of particularly rambunctious kids in the hall outside my class, I watched Mr. Davidson walk in and calmly ask to borrow Mrs. Alexander's meter stick. Apparently, the metric system just wasn't strong enough, because after some loud whipping sounds from outside Mr. Davidson came back with the stick broken in two, promising to order a new one. We heard later that he had beaten every kid in the hall. Not just the guilty kids, every kid. Authority had come, as violently, as indiscriminately, and as blindly as it was prone to. This was not a force you run to, one you count on to protect you; this is a force you run from. Its only desire was order and submission, and it didn't care if justice was the sacrifice. After that day, whenever I was standing in the vicinity of a group marked for discipline, I learned what I needed to do to survive: do not protest in any way, visibly submit my will utterly and completely so that the enforcer doesn't feel his authority threatened, forget pride and fairness, and hold on as long as it takes to find myself safely out of the situation. And I thank

God I could learn that lesson then, when dealing with a principal with a plywood measuring stick, long before I'd ever face cops with guns and billy clubs.

On the yard, there was no trustworthy figure to protect us, no larger, dependable force to impose order or intervene; this is much the same as it is in many black urban areas like Harlem. It was an entire power structure based on who could kick whose ass. Despite this flat-land version of "king of the hill" that the school bullies on the yard were engaged in daily, there were two ways of removing yourself from the ongoing power struggle. The first, and most popular, was sports. Every day there would be a handball game on the yard (we were too small for basketball), and every day participants in this game—out of some prepubescent testosterone-driven respect for another manly pur-suit—were given a free pass from having to fight. Some of the kids who learned this trick of using sports as a safety from the pressures of the black community continued with it up into high school, a special few even using it to go to college and beyond. For those who were ath-letically inept or indifferent, like myself, there was another option: hide. This could be as simple as locating the part of the yard with the most activity and getting as far away from it as possible, or taking advantage of havens like the library, safe in the knowledge that books repel the ignorant. I applied this same technique of concealment to the other dreaded time of chaos: after school. Completely unsupervised, we had to make our way home among all the other kids.

After school was the bad kids' finest moment. Plans for fights and bumrushes were drawn out all day for this golden hour. In response, I evolved my own plans of escape back to my apartment building. The most elaborate involved memorizing the R8 train schedule so that I could run down the tracks till I got closer to home. For further protec-tion, I would even wear a reversible jacket, which I would switch over to its barely used inside to try to confuse the predators looking for me in the crowd. At the time I thought this way of life, hiding from the bad people, would be a temporary one. But I was wrong. In areas prone to high crime, this is often the only way decent people can remove themselves from danger. Even today, I continue this life of avoidance and camouflage. Around Harlem, I wear the same baseball hat and bomber jacket, have that same street strut and way of talking as everyone else around me. Part of it is who I am, and part of it is about just disappearing into the crowd, trying not to appear like the one to be messed with. I like DKNY suits too, can speak academically as well as street, and sure as hell know how to walk straight, but when I'm going down Lenox, I don't want to do things that can make me look like a target. At night, for instance, instead of walking the seven blocks to my apartment from 125th Street Station, I pay the five bucks for the cab so I can be dropped off at my door. An annoying expense, yes, but just another necessary way of "hiding" that I and the majority of people in my neighborhood, decent people, do to protect themselves from the street-oriented minority who might make us their next victim if we chose to remain in plain sight.

By the end of second grade, despite my best efforts, trouble eventually tracked me down. That it came in the form of Tarrence Green should not be surprising. One minute I was playing *Six Million Dollar Man* in a little alcove behind the cafeteria with all the other nerds, making bionic noises with our mouths and moving in slow motion, and the next I was pushed to the ground with Tarrence standing over me.

"We gawn fight."

Who could argue with that logic? So simple, so brute, so true? I shouldn't have been surprised. It was just my turn, my time to show where I stood in the power structure. I was an attractive target as well: I was big for my age so that the matchup wouldn't seem as lopsided as it was, and had a smart mouth that would make my beating a surefire crowd-pleaser. Petrified and silently cursing the nonviolent resistance the Quakers had trained me for, I stood up and faced him, raising my fist the way I saw he was doing. And the funniest thing was, as every single kid on that yard swarmed in around us, steadily chanting their "Oooos" in a primitive chorus, I realized I was bigger than Tarrence. Right there, face-to-face, I could tell that, if I wanted to, I could reach out and smack Tarrence without him ever getting a hand on me. As I ducked his punches, I noticed that, damn, I was faster than he was, too. But just before I started getting cocky I thought, if I beat up Tarrence, he'll keep coming back for revenge every single day, trying to regain his pride and throne as the lord abuser. And if Tarrence couldn't do it, next he would bring his friends with them, and then their older brothers, until eventually I was outgunned. And if I swung on him, I would be suspended, and it would go on my permanent record and stop me from ever transferring out of this hellhole, and my mom would cut the cord on the TV again so there would be no cartoons for a month. But if Tarrence punched me, it would affect him in no way at all. My friends were wimps, and even though I had two older cousins at Houston, they were even bigger milquetoasts than I was. And Tarrence didn't care about his record; he already had so much ink on it that this incident would barely qualify for a footnote. He was failing the second grade, and it was doubtful his parents gave a damn. No, Tarrence had nothing to lose. If he punched me in the mouth it would just further solidify his school-yard prominence. So he did so, even as Mr. Davidson yanked him away from me.

That was the most amazing thing I learned all year. Being the biggest and baddest in this culture wasn't about innate pugilistic ability, or even how tough you were, it was about how far you were willing to go. How much you're willing to risk and how much you could afford to lose. Those with nothing always had something to gain, and were therefore willing to ignore any social or legal constraint in doing so. As we grew older, when guns became the great physical equalizer among my age group, this fact became even more obvious. The "strong" in this world were the people insane and hopeless enough to pull the trigger. The "weak" were the people who had something to live for.

I made it out of Houston eventually. Moved on to high school, sneaked into college, and learned to do well enough to get myself where I wanted in the world. But Henry H. Houston Elementary has never been that far away from me; the person I was then is probably the person I still see myself as now, even as my hair has grayed. I married a woman who is also a Houston alum, so it's not rare for me to get shaken awake with sentences starting with "Do you remember" followed by disbelief and incredulous laughter about that time.

But what's influenced my perspective on that time the most was an incident I had nearly a decade after I last stepped foot on Houston's yard. While in college, I was walking down Fifteenth and Market, visiting home after a yearlong exchange program in Britain, trying to buy a backpack for the monthlong trip around Europe I would be taking that spring. I was feeling good about myself too, about the opportunities I had bought myself by biding my time, taking my punches, and staying out of trouble, when I heard a voice yelling my name.

"Yo, Mat!" it kept saying frantically, and I turned around on the sidewalk to find its source, only to locate it from a vehicle on the street. It was Tarrence Green. He was so happy to see me, waving and screaming through the window of a school bus driving by. I waved back and thought, "Dear God, he never even graduated from the eighth grade." But it wasn't a school bus—they don't call them that when they have bars on the windows. PENNSYLVANIA STATE CORRECTION AUTHORITY was on the side. I could see the armed guard standing beside the driver, giving that look Mr. Davidson used to wear. At his window, hands seemingly bound, Tarrence waved hard, apparently remembering better times. He kept going, so I waved back to him, standing my ground until his bus turned its corner, driving Tarrence back toward whatever cinder-block institution was out there waiting for him.

POLICE STATE OF MIND

ROHAN PRESTON

My toddler daughter, who attracts smiles during our outings, humanizes me in the eyes of strangers. During our squeal-filled play in the Minneapolis Sculpture Garden or on singing bike rides around Minneapolis's chain of lakes, she usually receives approving greetings from a mosaic of passersby. She's curious and cute and I am proud and doting.

She draws warmth from people who might otherwise be guarded around me. The reactions that often register most deeply, however, come from African-American men. They reveal, in a hearty flash of teeth or lowered voice, approval, empathy, admiration, even hurt. And that's with strangers. Sometimes my daughter's presence evokes in my male friends and acquaintances (and also in me) a vulnerable openness and reflection that is otherwise hard to come by.

The most striking example of this, thus far, happened in the spring of 2000 at the Island Cuisine restaurant in Minneapolis. The Jamaican eatery, which usually feels more like a community center than a private establishment, serves as a gathering place for members of various social, fraternal, and charitable organizations who convene for business and pleasure.

One Saturday morning, when my then nearly three-year-old and I went to get a breakfast of ackee, codfish, and dumplings, I ran into a fellow member of my cricket team who is known both for bowling a ferocious pace (fast) ball and for his hair-trigger temper. He strutted over to our table.

As we made brief remarks about the previous week's game—he had demolished the wickets of a braggart from the opposing side—he zoomed in on my little girl. The pace bowler smiled as she quizzed him—her nearly recognizable words breaking the surface of language the way the skin of an alligator describes the surface of water—about his name and age, where he lived, and if he had a baby doll.

He just kept smiling.

In this, our first nonsport conversation in the two summers I had seen him at cricket games, he revealed that he had a son her age. I nodded with excitement, thinking, as usual, about playmates for my little girl. But the boy was in New York with his mother, he said. Because of an unspecified "situation," he could not be with his son.

I tried to encourage him, saying that I know how he must feel. But I did not know how he felt and had no desire to know that feeling. He seemed not to have heard me anyway. As he continued, he spoke less and less to me and more and more to himself. He mentioned his responsibilities to his son—how he wants to teach him to play cricket, to send him to college, how he missed his little boy. As my teammate continued speaking to me while looking at my daughter and thinking about his son, he tried to mute his emotions. But it was no use. He sounded wounded, his bruised voice tightening in his throat, his eyes reddening with grief. I clutched my daughter closer, trying to keep a bevy of nightmare scenarios at bay.

When we realized what was happening, we both straightened up and exchanged manly hugs. Though I am loath to show emotions in public, I was not afraid of tears that morning—mine or his—even in a restaurant that smelled of scotch bonnet peppers and thumped with chuckachucka dancehall music.

My recessed fear was on the surface of his reality. He seemed an unhelpful spectator stranded beyond his family's reach, like someone in an aquarium touching glass as fish suck air on the other side. I thought also of bees and wasps on the inside of windows, batting up against glass as they try to get out. I fret for such creatures, suspecting they will die as much from injury as from frustration, because they know that they could be on the outside, in air, breathing freely and contributing to the work of their kin.

I shuddered for the pace bowler and for me. Such an absence away from family, like being trapped by unforgiving glass, is a kind of death. And yet millions of people live it daily, finding ways to cope, hoping for resurrection. I just did not want to have that particular challenge.

The restaurant encounter pushed latent fears from my subconscious to the front of my mind. Could I be similarly separated—through imprisonment, through divorce, through death—from my family? Am I going to be killed by the police or someone else? My thoughts telescoped to those places of terror hanging over so many black men—the anonymous city morgues with their limitless supply of toe tags, the jail cells all across America waiting.

The whole thing made me anguished and reflective, roiling up uneasy thoughts about my own humanity that I ordinarily try to avoid. Amid our sniffles, I felt guardedly blessed.

I prayed for my cricket friend—for him to have closure, for him to have healing, for him to live.

Existential Paranoia

My existence, and that of many black men in America, is pressed between limiting, historical archetypes, on the one hand, and a de facto police state on the other. In this setup, which is overlaid with history, there's scant room for the rich spiritual, intellectual, and emotional experience that many cohorts and I have had. There's little room for an engaged aesthetic practice. So when the mold is broken, when my daughter allows people to see me as human, for example, it is a relief not just for passersby but also for me, even if it is seen as the exception that reinforces a rule.

Admittedly, my fears of forcible separation or death by police are not based on terrible things that I have suffered. My life has been made rich by an inspiring and loving blood family as well "family-in-the-large," as poet and humanitarian Gwendolyn Brooks liked to call dear friends.

My condition is born of vicarious experience. I have been soaking up the history and present. I voraciously read newspapers and magazines. I sometimes watch comedies and dramas. And I listen to a wide range of musical genres. From these sources, I have a sense of the low value of my life. I also have a sense of the depth of the dysfunction that I am supposed to represent and that I try to keep at bay like a wolf at the door, my broomstick in its mouth.

Because I am sentient and living in America, and because of what I have absorbed emotionally, intellectually, and through my pores—from science to the nightly television news—I know that it is not difficult to argue against my innocence in whatever situation. It is not difficult to argue that a black man in America—virtually any black man in America—is a criminal predator, a sick beast as otherworldly as King Kong or an alien movie monster busting through the floor. It is not difficult to argue that a black man—any black man—is a thing of such vileness and animality that he deserves, like Rodney King, a disciplined, rational response that might seem excessive only to those unfamiliar with the creature.

The lies that precede me have caused a certain dis-ease. I often feel that I must rebuke unspoken, low assumptions about my capacities as a person.

It is difficult to define this condition, which can be brought to the surface by the emotion of a friend or the wails of police sirens. It is not the crazed violence that Richard Wright so searingly noted in *Native Son* and *Black Boy*, the kind that can dislocate a person so much that he lashes out against oppression in an equally heinous way. This condition is only partly defined by the null-and-void humanity that Ralph Ellison wrote of in *Invisible Man*, the ghost existence that renders black men spectral shadows or holograms.

Nor is it a ponderous angst of uncertain source, like the inescapable paralyses in Samuel Beckett's minimalist dramas such as *Endgame* or *Happy Days*. And there's no unknowing wait here, for a Godot, somewhere out there.

The condition is a mix of existential paranoia and neurosis, all hanging in a mist that can quickly condense into a driving wall of terror. It exists in the present, for true, but it collapses the current and the historical. The conflation is most visible in how the police regard and deal with black men, as if we are unfree, as if we are fugitives from prisons or plantations.

I suspect that my dis-ease (and that of the culture around me) has to do with many unresolved, taboo subjects in our society, including the residue of slavery. Such topics immediately put people off (they are too painful for me as well). But even if they make us irrational—unable to hear or think clearly—they do not go away in the silence. They define, by shadow, our national situation, the one in which a black man becomes alternately a walking indictment that does not shrink away or someone on whom the culture can focus unexpiated guilt.

Regardless, our national condition recalls a dysfunctional household in which family members stay silent. The relations would rather ignore or deny the violations that hang over them. They would rather sulk, drink beer, and watch television instead, laughing all the way to the bathroom.

Police State

Our police do not tap phones and spread discrediting lies on a massive scale, like the prototypical governments of the old Eastern Europe, South America, or apartheid South Africa—though such things have been documented here. There's no known secret police in America, just uniformed and undercover officers. And their killings are not carried out in hidden torture chambers, but on the streets, randomly, all across the country, and often in plain sight.

The effect is just as chilling, and repressive, for black men in America.

There might be no national police conspiracy per se. But there need not be any formal codification. At this stage, it's a reflex. The templates are all there, hardwired, it seems, into our skulls and skins. The police know what they think they know about black men being criminals; any encounter with the police can mean your life.

If, say, during a twenty-five-dollar traffic stop, an officer should decide that my manners are not good enough, he can summarily end my life. If my wife and daughter are lucky, an official might issue a tepid apology—with raised shoulders and thrown-up hands. It would be a mistake, albeit a fatal one. And I would be faulted for disobedience, for resistance, for unlawful breathing. Although I have no previous encounter with criminal law, any traffic ticket I might have gotten would be dragged out to prove that I was of questionable humanity in the first place.

When I first read about Amadou Diallo, gunned down in a storm of forty-one bullets by four white undercover New York police officers, the inhumanity of the crime sickened me. I knew that even if Diallo had simply been taken out and shot by the police, it would have been rendered justifiable. I trembled, because that could have been me, returning late from work. Those undercover officers—who could have been night riders or a gang of thugs, for all this immigrant knew—had more rights over him than he had over his own body. They saw a predator, a rapist, a recalcitrant slave, not a man struggling with his English and his work. They did not see pedigree or heritage. They did not ask for his educational qualifications. They did not see him for the person he was, only as a menace, the shadowy figure they had been trained to kill.

Even if the riddling of Amadou Diallo were isolated, it would be difficult to rest easy. But it's part of a documented and widespread pattern. There are cases all over the continental United States of police killing innocent black men.

In New York, again, it happened in May 2000 to Haitian-born security guard Patrick Dorismond, who was approached on the street by a stranger seeking drugs. Dorismond took offense. The stranger turned out to be an undercover police officer. Dorismond's objection was met with a fatal bullet.

In Lebanon, Tennessee, it happened on October 4, 2000, as John Adams, a sixty-four-year-old retiree, sat in his tan recliner at home, watching television. Armed men invaded his home. He went for a weapon for protection. They shot him. He later died. Turned out they were police drug busters who had smashed in the door of the wrong house. A horrendous mistake. Sorry.

It seems it's just a matter of time before my number comes up.

Bob Marley sang, in "Slave Driver," "Every time I hear the crack of a whip, my blood runs cold." My own blood does not quite turn to mercury when I see policemen in my rearview mirror, but I always ask myself: Are my papers in order, have I used my indicator lights, is there anyone around to videotape this, just in case?

These encounters transport me to nightmares of reality police dramas, where I am guilty until proven innocent. I suss myself out, asking a battery of ridiculous questions and trying to keep my blood pressure in check: Did I kill/rape/rob anyone today? What harm have I done to society? Such encounters also take me into history, and I hear questions from a slavery subconscious: Who owns you? Do you have a pass to be here? Are you legal?

Though the knowledge that my life, valued at less than a sheet of newsprint, could be snuffed out at any time means that I live with a certain fear, I also have a certain freedom. I live a questioning, honest life. Though I have not fought in any wars, I know a few veterans who are unblinking truth tellers. I aspire to their courage.

I try to live with as much grace and humanity as I can, because, like it or not, I have to represent something and someone. The challenge is to not let this cloud of existential paranoia rain on me, to not become, for myself, an embodiment of others' fears and hatreds, a creature drawing the bitterness of others.

Breaking Character, Breaking Mold

Most men of color in America have a tenuous claim to full citizenship. Our rights are shaky, but not because we are not good, upstanding people. We are constructed to have very low expectations of ourselves— our abilities and capacities for deep intellectual, spiritual, and emotional growth. Thus our citizenship claim can be easily revoked at the slightest infraction—or jaywalking or not wearing a tie—without so much as a doubt.

Several years ago, I interviewed visual artist and storyteller Tom Feelings as he was irrigating a most painful and still-unresolved part of our history. He said that his twenty-year project to produce his highly evocative and wrenching book *The Middle Passage* came out of his revulsion for the way African captives are depicted in historical texts. They tend to be stick figures, packed like chicken bones into the hulls of slave ships. His mission was simple: illustrate human beings in a terrible situation.

His quest mirrors my own: to break the mold and mask of a representation of black men that does not allow for character development, for empathy; and to break the casting mold of our national narrative, where black men are usually slotted in roles such as the shadow lurking in the corner, the preternatural, hulking athlete who can do anything because of some captive breeding program, the singer delivering sweetness and light out of that very dark soul.

We have been cast in profile.

The roles are stock cutouts. When we demand something deeper, more substantive, when we move out of the shadows, audiences greet it as humorous or tragically comic. Most of our national directors, those whose policies guide our action, do not see us inhabiting center stage, except as jokes. Audiences, too, often cannot fathom a role out-side the set parameters. Yet African-American men inhabit them—often with grace and eloquence, with exemplary style, and affecting humanity.

When I hear the numbing statistics about the low numbers of black men matriculating in college versus the disproportionate num-bers of our brothers incarcerated across the country, when I hear about crimes and deaths, I do not absorb the numbers. I cannot. They are dots per inch, faceless, flat.

The data, which appear on the news with great regularity—as proof of problem rather than proof of need for help—work like a cor-rosive force field on me. I try to shed the load of these statistics, the negative gravity of it all, by being my richly individual and complex self: vulnerable, even-tempered, but okay with having moods. I try to be me with as little affectation as possible.

My quest is neither unique nor new. And it is a reaction against being measured according to the least capable of us, rather than by the refracted genius that has helped shape the culture of the globe. Indeed, the idea of black exceptionalism is so widely accepted by blacks and non-blacks alike that few question the notion that, once someone has made it, s/he has "transcended" race. Rubbish. Ellington, Coltrane, Bird—black in their bones. Ellison, Brooks, Morrison—these writers have shared genius as richly textured and colored as quilts because they have mined the soil of African America, finding gold in the shallows and depths and unfurling a banner to announce the common jewels. From Alvin Ailey, Trevor Rhone, and Judith Jamison to Chuck D, KRS-One, and DMX, we're not talking about isolation so much as the kind of heft that shifts the tectonic plates of culture, that moves mountains.

But the idea of a black exceptionalism that outstrips all negative or low expectations continues to rule. It manifests itself in myriad forms—from a Michael Jackson–like figure on the public stage to the everyday carriage of coworkers and fellow travelers who have to make them-selves as nonthreatening, with a robotlike equanimity, as possible.

The need not to be like all the other Negroes also shows up in the understandable attempt by so many African-Americans to identify as anything and everything but black. It is part of our long historic attempt to break free of the negative gravity that defines us by the worst among us.

The attempt to break out of the negative force field that traps us takes many forms. But it can be upended easily: by a clerk in a store who decides that we are an embodiment of criminality, by those we encounter daily who learned a different set of manners. These people are not difficult, though they create bumps along the way that have nothing to do with us.

All of my reasoning gets chiseled to a very fine point anywhere in America. The police, from the smallest town to New York City, can and do, for many random African-American men, routinely destroy every attempt to prove our worth. Officers in our rearview mirror, leering beside us, running our plates, always seem to raise Malcolm X's question: What is a Negro with a Ph.D.?

Marion McClinton, the fine director and playwright, says that he believes that African-Americans are among the most materialistic of Americans because we have an intimacy with capitalism that few have. "America is the best exemplar of capitalism and we know this system from its inception intimately," he says. "Our families were sold, so we know that if money could talk, it would tell us stories about ourselves, our history, our blood."

No matter how much we spend, we cannot buy our freedom, he said, though we might sometimes think of our already given gifts— innate and inalienable—as a commodity.

When we buy for styling and profiling, we are reenacting something deeper than the clothes or the cars or the homes. We're dealing in natal terrain, atavistic terrain, trying to undo the memory of what's been done, trying to bind a rupture, to reunite families.

Ultimately, we are trying to be fully human, to find affirmation in the face of denial and distortion, under the threat of erasure. I know we will prevail, not because we are righteous but because we are right, in our humanity, in our genius, in our love.

I first began to understand my differences—from the mainstream and other streams—when I was twelve. That is the age when I immigrated to Brooklyn from Jamaica. My father sat me down for a lecture on American culture. Even though I was not yet a teenager, he said, most people would treat me and expect me to react like an adult. I was to shoulder the responsibilities of manhood, prove him proud, and not do anything untoward. I had no idea what he was talking about and found my father's remarks alarmist, crazy, and out-of-touch.

I gradually grew to understand his concerns for my safety. And I grew to appreciate his advice about how to sound tough if anyone detained me during an errand and how to talk to the police with dignity and manners but to avoid offending them.

My father's love has been genuine and constant, even during our tumults. And I understand him better now.

I remember crying while talking to him on the phone the morning of my daughter's birth. I understood so much, at last, so overcome with joy that morning that it did not even register when my wife's obstetrician told me my newborn's gender.

Later, as I thought about lessons I had to teach her, I was relieved that I might not have to warn her against the police, though I quickly had a raft of other dangers to alert her to. My challenge is how to arm her without harming her—closing down her world, her possibilities, her dreams.

When my daughter and I read poems and stories, when we color and draw and write, it is with a certainty, and confidence in my wife, that even if I should disappear, my offspring will be armed with the grace to succeed. I want to equip her without hobbling her, to provide a platform from which she can spring.

Most parents have similar aspirations for their children. But given the conditions of our police state, given the litany of stuff arrayed against African-Americans, our dreams have a heightened urgency.

They occur in the reflections of knife blades and bullet tips. They grow out of the shadows of handcuffs and jail cells. They rise in the midst of coffins. But they will blossom yet, these dreams pressed between fears and threats. They will flower furiously, to again use the words of Gwendolyn Brooks, as my daughter and my cricket friend's son rise, their own dreams shimmering and shining, their own ambitions spiraling into the sky.

CONTRIBUTORS

JABARI ASIM is a poet, critic, and playwright who works as a senior editor of the *Washington Post Book World*. His work has appeared most recently in *Step Into a World: A Global Anthology of the New Black Literature*, *The Salon Reader's Guide to Contemporary Literature*, and *Brown Sugar: A Collection of Erotic Black Fiction*. He is also the author of *The Road to Freedom*, a novel for young adults.

CHRISTOPHER COOPER sits on the board of directors of the National Black Police Association. A former United States Marine and Washington, D.C., metropolitan police officer, he is an attorney. He has a Ph.D. and was a postdoctoral Fulbright Scholar (1996), having served at the University of Copenhagen, Denmark. He lectured and conducted research into interpersonal police conflict resolution methodologies. Dr. Cooper is an associate professor of sociology/criminal justice with a specialization in policing and conflict/dispute resolution at Saint Xavier University in Chicago. His publications include *Mediation & Arbitration by Patrol Police Officers* (University Press of America, 1999). Dr. Cooper is past chair of the Criminal Justice Sector for the Society of Professionals in Dispute Resolution and is a member of the National Association for Community Mediation.

RICARDO CORTEZ CRUZ is the author of *Straight Outta Compton* and *Five Days of Bleeding*. Winner of the Nilon Award for Excellence in Minority Fiction, *Straight Outta Compton* was hailed as "a violent, slangy, tour-de-force debut" by *Kirkus Reviews* and picked as one of 1992's best books by the *Nation*. Critics have called Cruz the first "rap novelist" and "the voice and raging energy of the ghetto." He has stitched together a third body of (s)language (or, [s]lang-guage), *Premature Autopsies: Tales of Darkest America*. His cultural work has appeared in numerous publications, including *New American Writing, Postmodern American Fiction: A Norton Anthology, Chicago Tribune*, the *Washington Post, American Book Review*, the *Iowa Review*, and, most recently, *Step Into a World: A Global Anthology of the New Black Literature*. Cruz teaches at Illinois State University.

Poet-writer BRIAN GILMORE was born and raised in Washington, D.C. Formerly a law reform attorney with the Washington Legal Clinic for the Homeless and the Neighborhood Legal Services Program, he still practices law in the District of Columbia. Gilmore is the author of two collections of poetry, *elvis presley is alive and well and living in harlem* (Third World Press, 1993) and *jungle nights and soda fountain rags: poem for duke ellington* (Karibu Books, 2000). His writings have appeared in the *Christian Science Monitor*, the *Nation*, the *Washington Afro-American*, and on *This American Life*.

E. LYNN HARRIS sold computers for thirteen years before quitting to write his first novel, *Invisible Life*. Failing to find a publisher, he published it himself in 1991 and sold it mostly at black-owned bookstores, beauty salons, and book clubs before he was "discovered" by Anchor Books. Anchor published *Invisible Life* as a trade paperback in 1994, and thus his career as an author was "officially" launched. *Invisible Life* was followed by *Just As I Am* (1994), *And This Too Shall Pass* (1996), and *If This World Were Mine* (1997), all published by Doubleday. *And*

This Too Shall Pass and *If This World Were Mine* were *New York Times* best-sellers for nine weeks and ten weeks, respectively. *Abide with Me*, published in March 1999, was also a *New York Times* best-seller. In 2000 Harris's sixth novel, *Not a Day Goes By*, debuted on the *New York Times* Bestseller list at #2. To date, Harris's novels have sold well over 1.5 million copies.

ANDRE JACKSON is a journalist born, raised, and currently residing in St. Louis, Missouri. He earned a B.S. in mass communications from Southern Illinois University-Edwardsville and an M.B.A. from Northwestern's Kellogg Graduate School of Management. He has worked as a reporter and editor at daily newspapers from Wilkes-Barre, Pennsylvania, to Kansas City, Missouri. Jackson's work has chronicled events ranging from a 2 Live Crew concert to a Ku Klux Klan rally. His work on race issues has earned honors from groups such as the National Association of Black Journalists and the Associated Press Managing Editors Association, as well as a lawsuit by an alleged grand genie of the KKK. He has written freelance pieces for a number of magazines and is currently threatening to write his own life story. Jackson lives with his wife, Lisa, two children, two cats, and mother-in-law.

MAT JOHNSON was born and raised in Philadelphia, and has since then lived elsewhere. He wrote a novel called *DROP*, which a lot of people liked, but of course some didn't. Luckily for him, the former were critics and the latter were morons. Mat's writing another one now, set in Harlem. In his personal life, Mat's basically happy. May we all be so lucky.

RM JOHNSON was born and raised in Chicago, Illinois. He spent five years in the U.S. Army before earning his degree in radiologic technology from the University of Louisiana at Monroe. RM began writing in 1990. His first novel, *The Harris Men*, was published by Simon & Schuster in 1999 and was met with critical acclaim. It appeared on the

Blackboard Bestseller list in both hardcover and paperback. His sophomore novel, *Father Found,* also critically praised, was published in April 2000. *The Harris Family,* the sequel to *The Harris Men,* will be released in fall 2001.

After a long, successful career living off his parents until age twenty-four, **FRED MCKISSACK JR.** went on to write *This Generation of Americans, Black Hoops,* and *Black Diamond,* three well-received sports books for children. He also spent eight years as a journalist, during which his work appeared in the *Progressive,* the *Washington Post,* and elsewhere. He currently lives with his understanding and upstanding wife in Milwaukee, where he works as a senior copywriter–brand strategist. However, he hopes to one day fulfill one of his two lifelong dreams and find work as a professional bullpen catcher or comic-book writer.

MARK ANTHONY NEAL is an assistant professor of English at the State University of New York at Albany, where he teaches courses in African-American cultural studies and critical theory. Neal is the author of *What the Music Said: Black Popular Music and Black Public Culture* and the forthcoming *Soul Babies: Black Popular Culture and the Post-Soul Aesthetic.* Neal resides in New York's capital district with his wife of nine years and their young daughter.

Poet and critic **ROHAN PRESTON** is author of the collection *Dreams in Soy Sauce,* and coeditor *Soulfires: Young Black Men on Love and Violence.* His poetry has been published in numerous anthologies and his literary accolades include the inaugural Henry Blakely Poetry Prize, given by Gwendolyn Brooks to honor her husband's memory. Jamaican-born, Brooklyn-reared, and Yale-educated, Preston has written for the *Chicago Tribune, New York Times,* and *Washington Post.* Since March 1998, he has been lead theater critic at the *Star Tribune* in Minneapolis, where he lives with his wife, the poet Angela Shannon, and their daughter.

DAVID DANTE TROUTT is a writer and professor of law at Rutgers Law. In 1998 he published *The Monkey Suit—and Other Short Fiction on African Americans and Justice* (The New Press), a collection of stories chronicling the imagined experiences of African-Americans involved in actual legal controversies from 1830 to the present. A 1991 graduate of Harvard Law School, he has practiced both public-interest and corporate law, advocating on a broad range of areas including inner-city economic development and intellectual property. His legal scholarship focuses on the law and theory of economic transformation in ghetto neighborhoods and the application of narrative methodology to racially sensitive issues, such as police brutality. In addition to publications analyzing poverty in California cities, Troutt's nonfiction work includes regular columns in the *Los Angeles Times*, *Code* magazine, and other periodicals. He lives in Brooklyn with his wife, Shawn.